Quotations from Chairman

MAO TSETUNG

Translation and edition by: D. Weinberg
Cover Design: J. Neuman

For information regarding special discounts for bulk purchases, please contact BN Publishing at info@bnpublishing.com

CONTENTS

Comrade Mao Tse-tung is the greatest Marxist-Leninist of our era. He has inherited, defended and developed Marxism-Leninism with genius, creatively and comprehensively, and has brought it to a higher and completely new stage.

Mao Tse-tung's thought is Marxism-Leninism of the era in which imperialism is heading for total collapse and socialism is advancing to world-wide victory. It is a powerful ideological weapon for opposing imperialism and for opposing revisionism and dogmatism. Mao Tse-tung's thought is the guiding principle for all the work of the Party, the army and the country.

Therefore, the most fundamental task in our Party's political and ideological work is at all times to hold high the great red banner of Mao Tse-tung's thought, to arm the minds of the people throughout the country with it and to persist in using it to command every field of activity. The broad masses of the workers, peasants and soldiers and the broad ranks of the revolutionary cadres and the intellectuals should really master Mao Tse-tung's thought; they should all study Chairman Mao's writings, follow his teachings, act according to his instructions and be his good fighters.

In studying the works of Chairman Mao, one should have specific problems in mind, study and apply his works in a creative way, combine study with application, first study what must be urgently applied so as to get quick results, and strive hard to apply what one is studying. In order really to master Mao Tse-tung's thought, it is essential to study many of Chairman Mao's basic concepts over and over again, and it is best to memorize important statements and study and apply them repeatedly. The newspapers should regularly carry quotations from Chairman Mao relevant to current issues for readers to study and apply.

The experience of the broad masses in their creative study and application of Chairman Mao's works in the last few years has proved that to study selected quotations from Chairman Mao with specific problems in mind is a good way to learn Mao Tse-tung's thought, a method conducive to quick results.

We have compiled Quotations from Chairman Mao Tse-tung in order to help the broad masses learn Mao Tse-tung's thought more effectively. In organizing their study, units should select passages that are relevant to the situation, their tasks, the current thinking of their personnel, and the state of their work.

In our great motherland, a new era is emerging in which the workers, peasants and soldiers are grasping Marxism-Leninism, Mao Tse-tung's thought. Once Mao Tse-tung's thought is grasped by the broad masses, it becomes an inexhaustible source of strength and a spiritual atom bomb of infinite power. The large-scale publication of Quotations from Chairman Mao Tse-tung is a vital measure for enabling the broad masses to grasp Mao Tse-tung's thought and for promoting the revolutionization of our people's thinking. It is our hope that all comrades will learn earnestly and diligently, bring about a new nation-wide high tide in the creative study and application of Chairman Mao's works, and, under the great red banner of Mao Tse-tung's thought, strive to build our country into a great socialist state with modern agriculture, modern industry, modern science and culture and modern national defence!

Lin Piao

1. THE COMMUNIST PARTY

The force at the core leading our cause forward is the Chinese Communist Party.

The theoretical basis guiding our thinking is Marxism-Leninism.

Opening address at the First Session of the First National People's Congress of the People's Republic of China (September 15, 1954).

If there is to be revolution, there must be a revolutionary party. Without a revolutionary party, without a party built on the Marxist-Leninist revolutionary theory and in the Marxist-Leninist revolutionary style, it is impossible to lead the working class and the broad masses of the people in defeating imperialism and its running dogs.

"Revolutionary Forces of the World Unite, Fight Against Imperialist Aggression!" (November 1948), Selected Works, Vol. IV, p. 284.

Without the efforts of the Chinese Communist Party, without the Chinese Communists as the mainstay of the Chinese people, China can never achieve independence and liberation, or industrialization and the modernization of her agriculture.

"On Coalition Government" (April 24, 1945), Selected Works, Vol. III, p. 318.

The Chinese Communist Party is the core of leadership of the whole Chinese people. Without this core, the cause of socialism cannot be victorious.

Talk at the general reception for the delegates to the Third National Congress of the New Democratic Youth League of China (May 25, 1957).

A well-disciplined Party armed with the theory of Marxism-Leninism, using the method of self-criticism and linked with the masses of the people; an army under the leadership of such a Party; a united front of all revolutionary classes and all revolutionary groups under the leadership of such a Party--these are the three main weapons with which we have defeated the enemy.

"On the People's Democratic Dictatorship" (June 30, 1949), Selected Works, Vol. IV, p. 422.

We must have faith in the masses and we must have faith in the Party. These are two cardinal principles. If we doubt these principles, we shall accomplish nothing.

Armed with Marxist-Leninist theory and ideology, the Communist Party of China has brought a new style of work to the Chinese people, a style of work which essentially entails integrating theory with practice, forging close links with the masses and practising self-criticism.

"On Coalition Government" (April 24, 1945), Selected Works, Vol. III, p. 314.

No political party can possibly lead a great revolutionary movement to victory unless it possesses revolutionary theory and a knowledge of history and has a profound grasp of the practical movement.

"The Role of the Chinese Communist Party in the National War" (October 1938), Selected Works, Vol. II, p. 208.

As we used to say, the rectification movement is "a widespread movement of Marxist education". Rectification means the whole Party studying Marxism through criticism and self-criticism. We can certainly learn more about Marxism in the course of the rectification movement.

Speech at the Chinese Communist Party's National Conference on Propaganda Work (March 12, 1957), 1st pocket ed., p. 14.

It is an arduous task to ensure a better life for the several hundred million people of China and to build our economically and culturally backward country into a prosperous and powerful one with a high level of culture. And it is precisely in order to be able to shoulder this task more competently and work better together with all non-Party people who are actuated by high ideals and determined to institute reforms that we must conduct rectification movements both now and in the future, and constantly rid ourselves of whatever is wrong.

Ibid. pp. 15-16.

Policy is the starting-point of all the practical actions of a revolutionary party and manifests itself in the process and the end-result of that party's actions. A revolutionary party is carrying out a policy whenever it takes any action. If it is not carrying out a correct policy, it is carrying out a wrong policy; if it is not carrying out a given policy consciously, it is doing so blindly. What we call experience is the process and the end-result of carrying out a policy. Only through the practice of the people, that is, through experience, can we verify whether a policy is correct or wrong and determine to what extent it is correct or wrong. But people's practice, especially the practice of a revolutionary party and the revolutionary masses, cannot but be bound up with one policy or another. Therefore, before any action is taken, we must explain the policy, which we have formulated in the light of the given circumstances, to Party members and to the masses. Otherwise, Party members and the masses will depart from the guidance of our policy, act blindly and carry out a wrong policy.

"On the Policy Concerning Industry and Commerce" (February 27, 1948), Selected Works, Vol. IV. pp. 204-5.

Our Party has laid down the general line and general policy of the Chinese revolution as well as various specific lines for work and specific policies. However, while many comrades remember our Party's specific lines for work and specific policies, they often forget its general line and general policy. If we actually forget the Party's general line and general policy, then we shall be blind, half-baked, muddle-headed revolutionaries, and when we carry out a specific line for work and a specific policy, we shall lose our bearings and vacillate now to the left and now to the right, and the work will suffer.

"Speech at a Conference of Cadres in the Shansi-Suiyuan Liberated Area" (April 1, 1948), Selected Works, Vol. IV, p. 238.

Policy and tactics are the life of the Party; leading comrades at all levels must give them full attention and must never on any account be negligent.

"A Circular on the Situation" (March 20, 1948), Selected Works, Vol. IV, p. 220.

2. CLASSES AND CLASS STRUGGLE

Classes struggle, some classes triumph, others are eliminated. Such is history; such is the history of civilization for thousands of years. To interpret history from this viewpoint is historical materialism; standing in opposition to this viewpoint is historical idealism.

"Cast Away Illusions, Prepare for Struggle" (August 14, 1949), Selected Works, Vol. IV, p. 428.

In class society everyone lives as a member of a particular class, and every kind of thinking, without exception, is stamped with the brand of a class.

"On Practice" (July 1937), Selected Works, Vol. I, p. 296.

Changes in society are due chiefly to the development of the internal contradictions in society, that is, the contradiction between the productive forces and the relations of production, the contradiction between classes and the contradiction between the old and the new; it is the development of these contradictions that pushes society forward and gives the impetus for the supercession of the old society by the new.

"On Contradiction" (August 1937), Selected Works, Vol. I, p. 314.

The ruthless economic exploitation and political oppression of the peasants by the landlord class forced them into numerous uprisings against its rule…It was the class struggles of the peasants, the peasant uprisings and peasant wars that constituted the real motive force of historical development in Chinese feudal society.

"The Chinese Revolution and the Chinese Communist Party" (December 1939), Selected Works, Vol. II, p. 308.

In the final analysis, national struggle is a matter of class struggle. Among the whites in the United States it is only the reactionary ruling circles who oppress the black people. They can in no way represent the workers, farmers, revolutionary intellectuals and other enlightened persons who comprise the overwhelming majority of the white people.

"Statement Supporting the American Negroes in Their Just Struggle Against Racial Discrimination by U.S. Imperialism" (August 8, 1963), People of the World, Unite and Defeat the U.S. Aggressors and All Their Lackeys, 2nd ed., pp. 3-4.

It is up to us to organize the people. As for the reactionaries in China, it is up to us to organize the people to overthrow them. Everything reactionary is the same; if you don't hit it, it won't fall. This is also like sweeping the floor; as a rule, where the broom does not reach, the dust will not vanish of itself.

"The Situation and Our Policy After the Victory in the War of Resistance Against Japan" (August 13, 1945), Selected Works, Vol. IV, p. 19.

The enemy will not perish of himself. Neither the Chinese reactionaries nor the aggressive forces of U.S. imperialism in China will step down from the stage of history of their own accord.

"Carry the Revolution Through to the End" (December 30, 1948), Selected Works, Vol. IV, p. 301.

A revolution is not a dinner party, or writing an essay, or painting a picture, or doing embroidery; it cannot be so refined, so leisurely and gentle, so temperate, kind, courteous, restrained and magnanimous. A revolution is an insurrection, an act of violence by which one class overthrows another.

"Report on an Investigation of the Peasant Movement in Hunan" (March 1927), Selected Works, Vol. I, p. 28.

Chiang Kai-shek always tries to wrest every ounce of power and every ounce of gain from the people. And we? Our policy is to give him tit for tat and to fight for every inch of land. We act after his fashion. He always tries to impose war on the people, one sword in his left hand and another in his right. We take up swords, too, following his example.... As Chiang Kai-shek is now sharpening his swords, we must sharpen ours too.

"The Situation and Our Policy After the Victory in the War of Resistance Against Japan" (August 13, 1945), Selected Works, Vol. IV, pp. 14-15.

Who are our enemies? Who are our friends? This is a question of the first importance for the revolution. The basic reason why all previous revolutionary struggles in China achieved so little was their failure to unite with real friends in order to attack real enemies. A revolutionary party is the guide of the masses, and no revolution ever succeeds when the revolutionary party leads them astray. To ensure that we will definitely achieve success in our revolution and will not lead the masses astray, we must pay attention to uniting with our real friends in order to attack our real enemies. To distinguish real friends from real enemies, we must make a general analysis of the economic status of the various classes in Chinese society and of their respective attitudes towards the revolution.

"Analysis of the Classes in Chinese Society" (March 1926), Selected Works, Vol. I, p. 13.

Our enemies are all those in league with imperialism--the warlords, the bureaucrats, the comprador class, the big Landlord class and the reactionary section of the intelligentsia attached to them. The leading force in our revolution is the industrial proletariat. Our closest friends are the entire semi-proletariat and petty bourgeoisie. As for the vacillating middle bourgeoisie, their right-wing may become our enemy and their left-wing may become our friend--but we must be constantly on our guard and not let them create confusion within our ranks.

Ibid. p. 19.

Whoever sides with the revolutionary people is a revolutionary. Whoever sides with imperialism, feudalism and bureaucrat-capitalism is a counter-revolutionary. Whoever sides with the revolutionary people in words only but acts otherwise is a revolutionary in speech. Whoever sides with the revolutionary people in deed as well as in word is a revolutionary in the full sense.

Closing speech at the Second Session of the First National Committee of the Chinese People's Political Consultative Conference (June 23, 1950).

I hold that it is bad as far as we are concerned if a person, a political party, an army or a school is not attacked by the enemy, for in that case it would definitely mean that we have sunk to the level of the enemy. It is good if we are attacked by the enemy since it proves that we have drawn a clear line of demarcation between the enemy and ourselves. It is still better if the enemy attacks us wildly and paints us as utterly black and without a single virtue; it demonstrates that we have not only drawn a clear line of demarcation between the enemy and ourselves but achieved a great deal in our work.

To Be Attacked by the Enemy Is Not a Bad Thing but a Good Thing (May 26, 1939), 1st pocket ed., p. 2.

We should support whatever the enemy opposes and oppose whatever the enemy supports.

"Interview with Three Correspondents from the Central News Agency, the Sao Tang Pao and the Hsin Min Pao" (September 16, 1939), Selected Works, Vol. II, p. 272.

Our stand is that of the proletariat and of the masses. For members of the Communist Party, this means keeping to the stand of the Party, keeping to Party spirit and Party policy.

"Talks at the Yenan Forum on Literature and Art" (May 1942), Selected Works, Vol. III, p. 70.

After the enemies with guns have been wiped out, there will still be enemies without guns; they are bound to struggle desperately against us, and we must never regard these enemies lightly. If we do nor now raise and understand the problem in this way, we shall commit the gravest mistakes.

"Report to the Second Plenary Session of the Seventh Central Committee of the Communist Party of China" (March 5, 1949), Selected Works, Vol. IV, p. 364.
The imperialists and domestic reactionaries will certainly not take their defeat lying down and they will struggle to the last ditch. After there is peace and order throughout the country, they will still engage in sabotage and create disturbances in various ways and will try every day and every minute to stage a comeback. This is inevitable and beyond all doubt, and under no circumstances must we relax our vigilance.

Opening address at the First Plenary Session of the Chinese People's Political Consultative Conference (September 21. 1949).

In China, although in the main socialist transformation has been completed with respect to the system of ownership, and although the large-scale and turbulent class struggles of the masses characteristic of the previous revolutionary periods have in the main come to an end, there are still remnants of the overthrown landlord and comprador classes, there is still a bourgeoisie, and the remolding of the petty bourgeoisie has only just started. The class struggle is by no means over. The class struggle between the proletariat and the bourgeoisie, the class struggle between the different political forces, and the class struggle in the ideological held between the proletariat and the bourgeoisie will continue to be long and tortuous and at times will even become very acute.

13

The proletariat seeks to transform the world according to its own world outlook, and so does the bourgeoisie. In this respect, the question of which will win out, socialism or capitalism, is still not really settled.

On the Correct Handling of Contradictions Among the People (February 27, 1957), 1st pocket ed., pp. 51-52.

It will take a fairly long period of time to decide the issue in the ideological struggle between socialism and capitalism in our country. The reason is that the influence of the bourgeoisie and of the intellectuals who come from the old society will remain in our country for a long time to come, and so will their class ideology. If this is not sufficiently understood, or is not understood at all, the gravest mistakes will be made and the necessity of waging the struggle in the ideological field will be ignored.

Ibid. pp. 52-53.

In our country bourgeois and petty-bourgeois ideology, anti-Marxist ideology, will continue to exist for a long time. Basically, the socialist system has been established in our country. We have won the basic victory in transforming the ownership of the means of production, but we have not yet won complete victory on the political and ideological fronts. In the ideological field, the question of who will win in the struggle between the proletariat and the bourgeoisie has not been really settled yet. We still have to wage a protracted struggle against bourgeois and petty-bourgeois ideology. It is wrong not to understand this and to give up ideological struggle. All erroneous ideas, all poisonous weeds, all ghosts and monsters, must be subjected to criticism; in no circumstance should they be allowed to spread unchecked. However, the criticism should be fully reasoned, analytical and convincing, and not rough, bureaucratic, metaphysical or dogmatic.

Speech at the Chinese Communist Party's National Conference on Propaganda Work (March 12, 1957), 1st pocket ed., pp. 26-27.

Both dogmatism and revisionism run counter to Marxism. Marxism must certainly advance; it must develop along with the development of practice and cannot stand still. It would become lifeless if it remained stagnant and stereotyped. However, the basic principles of Marxism must never be violated, or otherwise mistakes will be made. It is dogmatism to approach Marxism from a metaphysical point of view and to regard it as something rigid. It is revisionism to negate the basic principles of Marxism and to negate its universal truth. Revisionism is one form of bourgeois ideology. The revisionists deny the differences between socialism and capitalism, between the dictatorship of the proletariat and the dictatorship of the bourgeoisie. What they advocate is in fact not the socialist line but the capitalist line. In present circumstances, revisionism is more pernicious than dogmatism. One of our current important tasks on the ideological front is to unfold criticism of revisionism.

Ibid. pp. 27-28.

Revisionism, or Right opportunism, is a bourgeois trend of thought that is even more dangerous than dogmatism. The revisionists, the Right opportunists, pay lip service to Marxism; they too attack "dogmatism". But what they are really attacking is the quintessence of Marxism. They oppose or distort materialism and dialectics, oppose or try to weaken the people's democratic dictatorship and the leading role of the Communist Party, and oppose or try to weaken socialist transformation and socialist construction. After the basic victory of the socialist revolution in our country, there are still a number of people who vainly hope to restore the capitalist system and fight the working class on every front, including the ideological one. And their right-hand men in this struggle are the revisionists.

On the Correct Handling of Contradictions Among the People (February 27, 1957), 1st pocket ed., pp. 56-57.

3. SOCIALISM AND COMMUNISM

Communism is at once a complete system of proletarian ideology and a new social system. It is different from any other ideological and social system, and is the most complete, progressive, revolutionary and rational system in human history. The ideological and social system of feudalism has a place only in the museum of history. The ideological and social system of capitalism has also become a museum piece in one part of the world (in the Soviet Union), while in other countries it resembles "a dying person who is sinking fast, like the sun setting beyond the western hills", and will soon be relegated to the museum. The communist ideological and social system alone is full of youth and vitality, sweeping the world with the momentum of an avalanche and the force of a thunderbolt.

"On New Democracy" (January 1940), Selected Works, Vol. II, pp. 360-61.

The socialist system will eventually replace the capitalist system; this is an objective law independent of man's will. However much the reactionaries try to hold back the wheel of history, sooner or later revolution will take place and will inevitably triumph.

"Speech at the Meeting of the Supreme Soviet of the U.S.S.R. in Celebration of the 40th Anniversary of the Great October Socialist Revolution" (November 6, 1957).

We Communists never conceal our political views. Definitely and beyond all doubt, our future or maximum programme is to carry China forward to socialism and communism. Both the name of our Party and our Marxist world outlook unequivocally point to this supreme ideal of the future, a future of incomparable brightness and splendor.

"On Coalition Government" (April 24, 1945), Selected Works, Vol. III, p. 282.

Taken as a whole, the Chinese revolutionary movement led by the Communist Party embraces the two stages, i.e., the democratic and the socialist revolutions, which are two essentially different revolutionary processes, and the second process can be carried through only after the first has been completed. The democratic revolution is the necessary preparation for the socialist revolution, and the socialist revolution is the inevitable sequel to the democratic revolution. The ultimate aim for which all communists strive is to bring about a socialist and communist society.

"The Chinese Revolution and the Chinese Communist Party" (December 1939), Selected Works, Vol. II, pp. 330-31.

Socialist revolution aims at liberating the productive forces. The changeover from individual to socialist, collective ownership in agriculture and handicrafts and from capitalist to socialist ownership in private industry and commerce is bound to bring about a tremendous liberation of the productive forces. Thus the social conditions are being created for a tremendous expansion of industrial and agricultural production.

Speech at the Supreme State Conference (January 25, 1956).

We are now carrying out a revolution not only in the social system, the change from private to public ownership, but also in technology, the change from handicraft to large-scale modern machine production, and the two revolutions are interconnected. In agriculture, with conditions as they are in our country co-operation must precede the use of big machinery (in capitalist countries agriculture develops in a capitalist way). Therefore we must on no account regard industry and agriculture, socialist industrialization and the socialist transformation of agriculture as two separate and isolated things, and on no account must we emphasize the one and play down the other.

On the Question of Agricultural Co-operation (July 51, 1955), 3rd ed., pp. 19-20.

The new social system has only just been established and requires time for its consolidation. It must not be assumed that the new system can be completely consolidated the moment it is established, for that is impossible. It has to be consolidated step by step. To achieve its ultimate consolidation, it is necessary not only to bring about the socialist industrialisation of the country and persevere in the socialist revolution on the economic front, but to carry on constant and arduous socialist revolutionary struggles and socialist education on the political and ideological fronts. Moreover, various contributory international factors are required.

Speech at the Chinese Communist Party's National Conference on Propaganda Work (March 12, 1957), 1st pocket ed., p. 2.

In China the struggle to consolidate the socialist system, the struggle to decide whether socialism or capitalism will prevail, will still take a long historical period. But we should all realise that the new system of socialism will unquestionably be consolidated. We can assuredly build a socialist state with modern industry, modern agriculture, and modern science and culture.

Ibid. pp. 2-3.

The number of intellectuals who are hostile to our state is very small. They do not like our state, i.e., the dictatorship of the proletariat, and yearn for the old society. Whenever there is an opportunity they will stir up trouble and attempt to overthrow the Communist Party and restore the old China. As between the proletarian and the bourgeois roads, as between the socialist and the capitalist roads, these people stubbornly choose to follow the latter. In fact this road is impossible, and in fact, therefore, they are ready to capitulate to imperialism, feudalism and bureaucrat-capitalism. Such people are to be found in political circles and in industrial and commercial, cultural and educational, scientific and technological and religious circles, and they are extremely reactionary.

Ibid. pp. 3-4.

The serious problem is the education of the peasantry. The peasant economy is scattered, and the socialization of agriculture, judging by the Soviet Union's experience, will require a long time and painstaking work. Without socialization of agriculture, there can be no complete, consolidated socialism.

"On the People's Democratic Dictatorship" June 30, 1949), Selected Works, Vol. IV, p. 419.

We must have faith, first, that the peasant masses are ready to advance step by step along the road of socialism under the leadership of the Party, and second, that the Party is capable of leading the peasants along this road. These two points are the essence of the matter, the main current.

On the Question of Agricultural Co-operation (July 31, 1955), 3rd ed., p. 18.

The leading bodies in co-operatives must establish the dominant position of the poor peasants and the new lower middle peasants in these bodies, with the old lower middle peasants and the upper middle peasants--whether old or new--as the supplementary force. Only thus can unity between the poor and middle peasants be attained, the co-operatives be consolidated, production be expanded and the socialist transformation of the entire countryside be correctly accomplished in accordance with the Party's policy. Otherwise, unity between the middle and poor peasants cannot be attained, the co-operatives cannot be consolidated, production cannot be expanded, and the socialist transformation of the entire countryside cannot be achieved.

Introductory note to "How Control of the Wutang Co-operative Shifted from the Middle to the Poor Peasants" (1955), The Socialist Upsurge in China's Countryside, Chinese ed., Vol. II.

It is essential to unite with the middle peasants, and it is wrong not to do so. But on whom must the working class and the Communist Party rely in the countryside in order to unite with the middle peasants and realize the socialist transformation of the entire countryside? Surely on none other than the poor peasants. That was the case when the struggle against the landlords was being waged and the land reform was being carried out, and that is the case today when the struggle against the rich peasants and other capitalist elements is being waged to achieve the socialist transformation of agriculture. In both these revolutionary periods, the middle peasants wavered in the initial stages. It is only after they clearly see the general trend of events and the approaching triumph of the revolution that the middle peasants will come in on the side of the revolution. The poor peasants must work on the middle peasants and win them over, so that the revolution will broaden from day to day until final victory.

Introductory note to "The Lesson of the 'Middle-Peasant Cooperative' and the 'Poor-Peasant Co-operative' in Fuan County" (1955), The Socialist Upsurge in China's Countryside, Chinese ed., Vol. II.

There is a serious tendency towards capitalism among the well-to-do peasants. This tendency will become rampant if we in the slightest way neglect political work among the peasants during the co-operative movement and for a very long period after.

Introductory note to "A Resolute Struggle Must Be Waged Against the Tendency Towards Capitalism" (1955), The Socialist Upsurge in China's Countryside, Chinese ed., Vol. I.

The agricultural co-operative movement has been a severe ideological and political struggle from the very beginning. No cooperative can be established without going through such a struggle. Before a brand-new social system can be built on the site of the old, the site must be swept clean. Invariably, remnants of old ideas reflecting the old system remain in people's minds for a long time, and they do not easily give way. After a co-operative is established, it must go through many more struggles before it can be consolidated. Even then, the moment it relaxes its efforts it may collapse.

Introductory note to "A Serious Lesson" (1955), The Socialist Upsurge in China's Countryside, Chinese ed., Vol. I.

The spontaneous forces of capitalism have been steadily growing in the countryside in recent years, with new rich peasants springing up everywhere and many well-to-do middle peasants striving to become rich peasants. On the other hand, many poor peasants are still living in poverty for lack of sufficient means of production, with some in debt and others selling or renting out their land. If this tendency goes unchecked, the polarization in the countryside will inevitably be aggravated day by day. Those peasants who lose their land and those who remain in poverty will complain that we are doing nothing to save them from ruin or to help them overcome their difficulties. Nor will the well-to-do middle peasants who are heading in the capitalist direction be pleased with us, for we shall never be able to satisfy their demands unless we intend to take the capitalist road. Can the worker-peasant alliance continue to stand him in these circumstances? Obviously not. There is no solution to this problem except on a new basis. And that means to bring about, step by step, the socialist transformation of the whole of agriculture simultaneously with the gradual realization of socialist industrialization and the socialist transformation of handicrafts and capitalist industry and commerce; in other words, it means to carry out co-operation and eliminate the rich-peasant economy and the individual economy in the countryside so that all the rural people will become increasingly well off together. We maintain that this is the only way to consolidate the worker-peasant alliance.

On the Question of Agricultural Co-operation (July 31, 1955), 3rd ed., pp. 26-27.

By over-all planning we mean planning which takes into consideration the interests of the 600 million people of our country. In drawing up plans, handling affairs or thinking over problems, we must proceed from the fact that China has a population of 600 million people, and we must never forget this fact.

On the Correct Handling of Contradictions Among the People (February 27, 1957), 1st pocket ed. p. 47.

In addition to the leadership of the Party, a decisive factor is our population of 600 million. More people mean a greater ferment of ideas, more enthusiasm and more energy. Never before have the masses of the people been so inspired, so militant and so daring as at present.

"Introducing a Co-operative" (April 15, 1958).

Apart from their other characteristics, the outstanding thing about China's 600 million people is that they are "poor and blank". This may seem a bad thing, but in reality it is a good thing. Poverty gives rise to the desire for change, the desire for action and the desire for revolution. On a blank sheet of paper free from any mark, the freshest and most beautiful characters can be written, the freshest and most beautiful pictures can be painted.

Ibid.

After the countrywide victory of the Chinese revolution and the solution of the land problem, two basic contradictions will still exist in China. The first is internal, that is, the contradiction between the working class and the bourgeoisie. The second is external; that is, the contradiction between China and the imperialist countries. Consequently, after the victory of the people's democratic revolution, the state power of the people's Republic under the leadership of the working class must not be weakened but must be strengthened.

"Report to the Second Plenary Session of the Seventh Central Committee of the Communist Party of China" (March 5, 1949), Selected Works, Vol. IV, p. 369.

"Don't you want to abolish state power?" Yes, we do, but not right now; we cannot do it yet. Why? Because imperialism still exists, because domestic reaction still exists, because classes still exist in our country. Our present task is to strengthen the people's state apparatus--mainly the people's army, the people's police and the people's courts--in order to consolidate national defence and protect the people's interests.

"On the People's Democratic Dictatorship" (June 30, 1949), Selected Works, Vol. IV, p. 418.

Our state is a people's democratic dictatorship led by the working class and based on the worker-peasant alliance. What is this dictatorship for? Its first function is to suppress the reactionary classes and elements and those exploiters in our country who resist the socialist revolution, to suppress those who try to wreck our socialist construction, or in other words, to resolve the internal contradictions between ourselves and the enemy. For instance, to arrest, try and sentence certain counterrevolutionaries, and to deprive landlords and bureaucrat-capitalists of their right to vote and their freedom of speech for a specified period of time--all this comes within the scope of our dictatorship. To maintain public order and safeguard the interests of the people, it is likewise necessary to exercise dictatorship over embezzlers, swindlers, arsonists, murderers, criminal gangs and other scoundrels who seriously disrupt public order. The second function of this dictatorship is to protect our country from subversion and possible aggression by external enemies. In that event, it is the task of this dictatorship to resolve the external contradiction between ourselves and the enemy. The aim of this dictatorship is to protect all our people so that they can devote themselves to peaceful labour and build China into a socialist country with a modern industry, agriculture, science and culture.

On the Correct Handling of Contradictions Among the People (February 27, 1957), 1st pocket ed., pp. 6-7.

The people's democratic dictatorship needs the leadership of the working class, for it is only the working class that is most far-sighted, most selfless and most thoroughly revolutionary. The entire history of revolution proves that without the leadership of the working class revolution fails and that with the leadership of the working class revolution triumphs.

"On the People's Democratic Dictatorship" (June 30, 1949), Selected Works, Vol. IV, p. 421.

The people's democratic dictatorship is based on the alliance of the working class, the peasantry and the urban petty bourgeoisie, and mainly on the alliance of the workers and the peasants, because these two classes comprise 80 to 90 per cent of China's population. These two classes are the main force in overthrowing imperialism and the Kuomintang reactionaries. The transition from New Democracy to socialism also depends mainly upon their alliance.

Ibid.

Class struggle, the struggle for production and scientific experiment are the three great revolutionary movements for building a mighty socialist country. These movements are a sure guarantee that Communists will be free from bureaucracy and immune against revisionism and dogmatism, and will forever remain invincible. They are a reliable guarantee that the proletariat will be able to unite with the broad working masses and realize a democratic dictatorship. If, in the absence of these movements, the landlords, rich peasants, counterrevolutionaries, bad elements and monsters were all allowed to crawl out, while our cadres were to shut their eyes to all this and in many cases fail even to differentiate between the enemy and ourselves but were to collaborate with the enemy and were corrupted, divided and demoralized by him, if our cadres were thus pulled out or the enemy were able to sneak in, and if many of our workers, peasants, and intellectuals were left defenceless against both the soft and the hard tactics of the enemy, then it would not take long, perhaps only several years or a decade, or several decades at most, before a counterrevolutionary restoration on a national scale inevitably occurred, the Marxist-Leninist party would undoubtedly become a revisionist party or a fascist party, and the hole of China would change its colour.

Note on "The Seven Well-Written Documents of Chekiang Province Concerning Cadres' Participation in Physical Labour" (May 9, 1963), quoted in On Khrushchov's Phoney Communism and Its Historical Lessons for the World, pp. 71-72.

The people's democratic dictatorship uses two methods. Towards the enemy, it uses the method of dictatorship, that is, for as long a period of time as is necessary it does not let them take part in political activities and compels them to obey the law of the People's Government and to engage in labour and, through labour, transform themselves into new men. Towards the people, on the contrary, it uses the method not of compulsion but of democracy, that is, it must necessarily let them take part in political activities and does not compel them to do this or that, but uses the method of democracy in educating and persuading them.

Closing speech at the Second Session of the First National Committee of the Chinese People's Political Consultative Conference (June 23, 1950).

Under the leadership of the Communist Party, the Chinese people are carrying out a vigorous rectification movement in order to bring about the rapid development of socialism in China on a firmer basis. It is a movement for carrying out a nation-wide debate which is both guided and free, a debate in the city and the countryside on such questions as the socialist road versus the capitalist road, the basic system of the state and its major policies, the working style of Party and government functionaries, and the question of the welfare of the people, a debate which is conducted by setting forth facts and reasoning things out, so as correctly to resolve those actual contradictions among the people which demand immediate solution. This is a socialist movement for the self-education and self-remolding of the people.

"Speech at the Meeting of the Supreme Soviet of the U.S.S.R. in Celebration of the 40th Anniversary of the Great October Socialist Revolution" (November 6, 1957)

Most arduous tasks lie ahead of us in the great work of construction. Although there are over 10 million members in our Party, they still constitute a very small minority of the country's population. In government departments and public organizations and enterprises much work has to be done by non-Party people. It is impossible to get this work well done unless we are good at relying on the masses and co-operating with non-Party people. While continuing to strengthen the unity of the whole Party, we must also continue to strengthen the unity of all our nationalities, democratic classes, democratic parties and people's organizations, and to consolidate and expand the people's democratic united front, and we must conscientiously get rid of every unhealthy manifestation in any link in our work that is detrimental to the unity between the Party and the people.

"Opening Address at the Eighth National Congress of the Communist Party of China" (September 15, 1956).

4. THE CORRECT HANDLING OF CONTRADICTIONS AMONG THE PEOPLE

We are confronted by two types of social contradictions--those between ourselves and the enemy and those among the people themselves. The two are totally different in their nature.

On the Correct Handling of Contradictions Among the People (February 27, 1957), 1st pocket ed. p. 2.

To understand these two different types of contradictions correctly, we must first be clear on what is meant by "the people", and what is meant by "the enemy". At the present stage, the period of building socialism, the classes, strata and social groups which favour, support and work for the cause of socialist construction all come within the category of the people, while the social forces and groups which resist the socialist revolution and are hostile to or sabotage socialist construction are all enemies of the people.

Ibid. pp. 2-3.

In the conditions prevailing in China today, the contradictions among the people comprise the contradictions within the working class, the contradictions within the peasantry, the contradictions within the intelligentsia, the contradictions between the working class and the peasantry, the contradictions between the workers and peasants on the one hand and the intellectuals on the other, the contradictions between the working class and other sections of the working people on the one hand and the national bourgeoisie on the other, the contradictions within the national bourgeoisie, and so on. Our People's Government is one that genuinely represents the people's interests; it is a government that serves the people. Nevertheless, there are still certain contradictions between the government and the people. These include contradictions among the interests of the state, the interests of the collective and the interests of the individual; between democracy and centralism; between the leadership and the led; and the contradiction arising from the bureaucratic style of work of certain government workers in their relations with the masses. All these are also contradictions among the people. Generally speaking, the people's basic identity of interests underlies the contradictions among the people.
Ibid. pp. 3-4.

The contradictions between ourselves and the enemy are antagonistic contradictions. Within the ranks of the people, the contradictions among the working people are non-antagonistic, while those between the exploited and the exploiting classes have a non-antagonistic aspect in addition to an antagonistic aspect.

Ibid. p. 3.

In the political life of our people, how should right be distinguished from wrong in one's words and actions? On the basis of the principles of our Constitution, the will of the overwhelming majority of our people and the common political positions which have been proclaimed on various occasions by our political parties and groups, we consider that, broadly speaking, the criteria should be as follows:

(1) Words and actions should help to unite, and not divide, the people of our various nationalities.

(2) They should be beneficial, and not harmful, to socialist transformation and socialist construction.
(3) They should help to consolidate, and not undermine or weaken, the people's democratic dictatorship.
(4) They should help to consolidate, and not undermine or weaken, democratic centralism.
(5) They should help to strengthen, and not discard or weaken, the leadership of the Communist Party.
(6) They should be beneficial, and not harmful, to international socialist unity and the unity of the peace-loving people of the world.

Of these six criteria, the most important are the socialist path and the leadership of the Party.

Ibid. pp. 57-58.

The question of suppressing counterrevolutionaries is one of a struggle between ourselves and the enemy, a contradiction between ourselves and the enemy. Among the people, there are some who see this question in a somewhat different light. Two kinds of persons hold views different from ours. Those with a Rightist way of thinking make no distinction between ourselves and the enemy and take the enemy for our own people. They regard as friends the very persons whom the broad masses regard as enemies. Those with a "Left" way of thinking magnify contradictions between ourselves and the enemy to such an extent that they take certain contradictions among the people for contradictions with the enemy and regard as counter-revolutionary persons who are actually not counter-revolutionaries. Both these views are wrong. Neither can lead to the correct handling of the question of suppressing counter-revolutionaries or to a correct assessment of this work.

Ibid. p. 25.

Qualitatively different contradictions can only be resolved by qualitatively different methods. For instance, the contradiction between the proletariat and the bourgeoisie is resolved by the method of socialist revolution; the contradiction between the great masses of the people and the feudal system is resolved by the method of democratic revolution; the contradiction between the colonies and imperialism is resolved by the method of national revolutionary war; the contradiction between the working class and the peasant class in socialist society is resolved by the method of collectivization and mechanization in agriculture; contradiction within the Communist Party is resolved by the method of criticism and self-criticism; the contradiction between society and nature is resolved by the method of developing the productive forces. The principle of using different methods to resolve different contradictions is one which Marxist-Leninists must strictly observe.

"On Contradiction" (August 1937), Selected Works, Vol. I, pp. 321-22.

Since they are different in nature, the contradictions between ourselves and the enemy and the contradictions among the people must be resolved by different methods. To put it briefly, the former are a matter of drawing a clear distinction between ourselves and the enemy, and the latter a matter of drawing a clear distinction between right and wrong. It is, of course, true that the distinction between ourselves and the enemy is also a matter of right and wrong. For example, the question of who is in the right, we or the domestic and foreign reactionaries, the imperialists, the feudalists and bureaucrat-capitalists, is also a matter of right and wrong, but it is in a different category from questions of right and wrong among the people.

On the Correct Handling of Contradictions Among the People (February 27, 1957), 1st pocket ed., pp. 5-6.

The only way to settle questions of an ideological nature or controversial issues among the people is by the democratic method, the method of discussion, of criticism, of persuasion and education, and not by the method of coercion or repression.

To be able to carry on their production and studies effectively and to arrange their lives properly, the people want their government and those in charge of production and of cultural and educational organizations to issue appropriate orders of an obligatory nature. It is common sense that the maintenance of public order would be impossible without such administrative regulations. Administrative orders and the method of persuasion and education complement each other in resolving contradictions among the people. Even administrative regulations for the maintenance of public order must be accompanied by persuasion and education, for in many cases regulations alone will not work.

Ibid. pp. 11-12.

Inevitably, the bourgeoisie and petty bourgeoisie will give expression to their own ideologies. Inevitably, they will stubbornly express themselves on political and ideological questions by every possible means. You cannot expect them to do otherwise. We should not use the method of suppression and prevent them from expressing themselves, but should allow them to do so and at the same time argue with them and direct appropriate criticism at them. We must undoubtedly criticize wrong ideas of every description. It certainly would not be right to refrain from criticism, look on while wrong ideas spread unchecked and allow them to monopolize the field. Mistakes must be criticized and poisonous weeds fought wherever they crop up. However, such criticism should not be dogmatic, and the metaphysical method should not be used, but efforts should be made to apply the dialectical method. What is needed is scientific analysis and convincing argument.

Ibid. pp. 55-56.

To criticize the people's shortcomings is necessary, but in doing so we must truly take the stand of the people and speak out of whole-hearted eagerness to protect and educate them. To treat comrades like enemies is to go over to the stand of the enemy.

"Talks at the Yenan Forum on Literature and Art" (May 1942), Selected Works, Vol. III, p. 92.

Contradiction and struggle are universal and absolute, but the methods of resolving contradictions, that is, the forms of struggle, differ according to the differences in the nature of the contradictions. Some contradictions are characterized by open antagonism; others are not. In accordance with the concrete development of things, some contradictions which were originally non-antagonistic develop into antagonistic ones, while others which were originally antagonistic develop into non-antagonistic ones.

"On Contradiction" (August 1937), Selected Works, Vol. I, p. 344.

In ordinary circumstances, contradictions among the people are not antagonistic. But if they are not handled properly, or if we relax our vigilance and lower our guard, antagonism may arise. In a socialist country, a development of this kind is usually only a localized and temporary phenomenon. The reason is that the system of exploitation of man by man has been abolished and the interests of the people are basically the same.

On the Correct Handling of Contradictions Among the People (February 27, 1957), 1st pocket ed., p. 14.

In our country, the contradiction between the working class and the national bourgeoisie belongs to the category of contradictions among the people. By and large, the class struggle between the two is a class struggle within the ranks of the people, because the Chinese national bourgeoisie has a dual character. In the period of the bourgeois-democratic revolution, it had both a revolutionary and a conciliationist side to its character. In the period of the socialist revolution, exploitation of the working class for profit constitutes one side of the character of the national bourgeoisie, while its support of the Constitution and its willingness to accept socialist transformation constitute the other. The national bourgeoisie differs from the imperialists, the landlords and the bureaucrat-capitalists. The contradiction between the national bourgeoisie and the working class is one between the exploiter and the exploited, and is by nature antagonistic. But in the concrete conditions of China, this antagonistic class contradiction can, if properly handled, be transformed into a non-antagonistic one and be resolved by peaceful methods. However, it will change into a contradiction between ourselves and the enemy if we do not handle it properly and do not follow the policy of uniting with, criticizing and educating the national bourgeoisie, or if the national bourgeoisie does not accept this policy of ours.

Ibid. p. 4-5.

It [the counter-revolutionary rebellion in Hungary in 1956] was a case of reactionaries inside a socialist country, in league with the imperialists, attempting to achieve their conspiratorial aims by taking advantage of contradictions among the people to foment dissension and stir up disorder. This lesson of the Hungarian events merits attention.

Ibid. p. 15.

5. WAR AND PEACE

War is the highest form of struggle for resolving contradictions, when they have developed to a certain stage, between classes, nations, states, or political groups, and it has existed ever since the emergence of private property and of classes.

"Problems of Strategy in China's Revolutionary War" (December 1936), Selected Works, Vol. I, p. 180.

"War is the continuation of politics." In this sense war is politics and war itself is a political action; since ancient times there has never been a war that did not have a political character...But war has its own particular characteristics and in this sense it cannot be equated with politics in general. "War is the continuation of politics by other means." When politics develops to a certain stage beyond which it cannot proceed by the usual means, war breaks out to sweep the obstacles from the way. When the obstacle is removed and our political aim attained the war will stop. But if the obstacle is not completely swept away, the war will have to continue till the aim is fully accomplished.... It can therefore be said that politics is war without bloodshed while war is politics with bloodshed.

"On Protracted War" (May 1938), Selected Works, Vol. II, pp. 152-53

History shows that wars are divided into two kinds, just and unjust. All wars that are progressive are just, and all wars that impede progress are unjust. We Communists oppose all unjust wars that impede progress, but we do not oppose progressive, just wars. Not only do we Communists not oppose just wars, we actively participate in them. As for unjust wars, World War I is an instance in which both sides fought for imperialist interests; therefore the Communists of the whole world firmly opposed that war. The way to oppose a war of this kind is to do everything possible to prevent it before it breaks out and, once it breaks out, to oppose war with war, to oppose unjust war with just war, whenever possible.

Ibid. p. 150.

Revolutions and revolutionary wars are inevitable in class society, and without them it is impossible to accomplish any leap in social development and to overthrow the reactionary ruling classes and therefore impossible for the people to win political power.

"On Contradiction" (August1937), Selected Works, Vol. I, p. 344.*

Revolutionary war is an anti-toxin which not only eliminates the enemy's poison but also purges us of our own filth. Every just, revolutionary war is endowed with tremendous power and can transform many things or clear the way for their transformation. The Sino-Japanese war will transform both China and Japan; provided China perseveres in the War of Resistance and in the united front, the old Japan will surely be transformed into a new Japan and the old China into a new China, and people and everything else in both China and Japan will be transformed during and after the war.

"On Protracted War" (May 1938), Selected Works, Vol. II, p. 131.

Every Communist must grasp the truth, "Political power grows out of the barrel of a gun."

"Problems of War and Strategy" (November 6, 1938), Selected Works, Vol. II, p. 224.

The seizure of power by armed force, the settlement of the issue by war, is the central task and the highest form of revolution. This Marxist-Leninist principle of revolution holds good universally, for China and for all other countries.

Ibid. p. 219.

Without armed struggle neither the proletariat, nor the people, nor the Communist Party would have any standing at all in China and it would be impossible for the revolution to triumph. In these years [the eighteen years since the founding of the Party] the development, consolidation and bolshevization of our Party have proceeded in the midst of revolutionary wars; without armed struggle the Communist Party would assuredly not be what it is today. Comrades throughout the Party must never forget this experience for which we have paid in blood.

Introducing The Communist" (October 4, 1939), Selected Works, Vol. II, p. 292.

According to the Marxist theory of the state, the army is the chief component of state power. Whoever wants to seize and retain state power must have a strong army. Some people ridicule us as advocates of the "omnipotence of war". Yes, we are advocates of the omnipotence of revolutionary war; that is good, not bad; it is Marxist. The guns of the Russian Communist Party created socialism. We shall create a democratic republic. Experience in the class struggle in the era of imperialism teaches us that it is only by the power of the gun that the working class and the labouring masses can defeat the armed bourgeoisie and landlords; in this sense we may say that only with guns can the whole world be transformed.

"Problems of War and Strategy" (November 6, 1938), Selected Works, Vol. II, p. 225.

We are advocates of the abolition of war, we do not want war; but war can only be abolished through war, and in order to get rid of the gun it is necessary to take up the gun.

Ibid.

War, this monster of mutual slaughter among men, will be finally eliminated by the progress of human society, and in the not too distant future too. But there is only one way to eliminate it and that is to oppose war with war, to oppose counter-revolutionary war with revolutionary war, to oppose national counter-revolutionary war with national revolutionary war, and to oppose counter-revolutionary class war with revolutionary class war. When human society advances to the point where classes and states are eliminated, there will be no more wars, counter-revolutionary or revolutionary, unjust or just; that will be the era of perpetual peace for mankind. Our study of the laws of revolutionary war springs from the desire to eliminate all wars; herein lies the distinction between us Communists and all the exploiting classes.

"Problems of Strategy in China's Revolutionary War" (December 1936), *Selected Works, Vol. I*, pp. 182-83.

Our country and all the other socialist countries want peace; so do the peoples of all the countries of the world. The only ones who crave war and do not want peace are certain monopoly capitalist groups in a handful of imperialist countries which depend on aggression for their profits.

"Opening Address at the Eighth National Congress of the Communist Party of China" (September 15, 1956).

To achieve a lasting world peace, we must further develop our friendship and co-operation with the fraternal countries in the socialist camp and strengthen our solidarity with all peace-loving countries. We must endeavour to establish normal diplomatic relations, on the basis of mutual respect for territorial integrity and sovereignty and of equality and mutual benefit, with all countries willing to live together with us in peace. We must give active support to the national independence and liberation movement in countries in Asia, Africa and Latin America as well as to the peace movement and to just struggles in all the countries of the world.

Ibid.

As for the imperialist countries, we should unite with their peoples and strive to coexist peacefully with those countries, do business with them and prevent any possible war, but under no circumstances should we harbour any unrealistic notions about them.

On the Correct Handling of Contradictions Among the People (February 27, 1957), 1st pocket ed., p. 75.

We desire peace. However, if imperialism insists on fighting a war, we will have no alternative but to take the firm resolution to fight to the finish before going ahead with our construction. If you are afraid of war day in day out, what will you do if war eventually comes? First I said that the East Wind is prevailing over the West Wind and war will not break out, and now I have added these explanations about the situation in case war should break out. Both possibilities have thus been taken into account.

Speech at the Moscow Meeting of Communist and Workers' Parties (November 18, 1957), quoted in "Statement by the Spokesman of the Chinese Government" (September 1, 1963).

People all over the world are now discussing whether or not a third world war will break out. On this question, too, we must be mentally prepared and do some analysis. We stand firmly for peace and against war. But if the imperialists insist on unleashing another war, we should not be afraid of it. Our attitude on this question is the same as our attitude towards any disturbance: first, we are against it; second, we are not afraid of it. The First World War was followed by the birth of the Soviet Union with a population of 200 million. The Second World War was followed by the emergence of the socialist camp with a combined population of 900 million. If the imperialists insist on launching a third world war, it is certain that several hundred million more will turn to socialism, and then there will not be much room left on earth for the imperialists; it is also likely that the whole structure of imperialism will utterly collapse.

On the Correct Handling of Contradictions Among the People (February 27, 1957), 1st pocket ed., pp. 67-68.

Make trouble, fail, make trouble again, fail again...till their doom--that is the logic of the imperialists and all reactionaries the world over in dealing with the people's cause, and they will never go against this logic. This is a Marxist law. When we say "imperialism is ferocious", we mean that its nature will never change, that the imperialists will never lay down their butcher knives, that they will never become Buddhas, till their doom.

Fight, fail, fight again, fail again, fight again...till their victory; that is the logic of the people, and they too will never go against this logic. This is another Marxist law. The Russian people's revolution followed this law, and so has the Chinese people's revolution.

"Cast Away Illusions, Prepare for Struggle" (August 14, 1949), Selected Works, Vol. IV, p. 428.
Just because we have won victory, we must never relax our vigilance against the frenzied plots for revenge by the imperialists and their running dogs. Whoever relaxes vigilance will disarm himself politically and land himself in a passive position.

"Address to the Preparatory Committee of the New Political Consultative Conference" (June 15, 1949), Selected Works, Vol. IV, p. 407.

The imperialists and their running dogs, the Chinese reactionaries, will not resign themselves to defeat in this land of China. They will continue to gang up against the Chinese people in every possible way. For example, they will smuggle their agents into China to sow dissension and make trouble. That is certain; they will never neglect these activities. To take another example, the imperialists will incite the Chinese reactionaries, and even throw in their own forces, to blockade China's ports. They will do this as long as it is possible. Furthermore, if they still hanker after adventures, they will send some of their troops to invade and harass China's frontiers; this, too, is not impossible. All this we must take fully into account.

Ibid.

The world is progressing, the future is bright and no one can change this general trend of history. We should carry on constant propaganda among the people on the facts of world progress and the bright future ahead so that they will build their confidence in victory.

"On the Chungking Negotiations" (October 17, 1945), Selected Works, Vol. IV. p. 59.

The commanders and fighters of the entire Chinese People's Liberation Army absolutely must not relax in the least their will to fight; any thinking that relaxes the will to fight and belittles the enemy is wrong.

"Report to the Second Plenary Session of the Seventh Central Committee of the Communist Party of China" (March 5, 1949), Selected Works, Vol. IV, p. 361.

6. IMPERIALISM AND ALL REACTIONARIES ARE PAPER TIGERS

All reactionaries are paper tigers. In appearance, the reactionaries are terrifying, but in reality they are not so powerful. From a long-term point of view, it is not the reactionaries but the people who are really powerful.

"Talk with the American Correspondent Anna Louise Strong" (August 1946), Selected Works, Vol. IV, p. 100.

Just as there is not a single thing in the world without a dual nature (this is the law of the unity of opposites), so imperialism and all reactionaries have a dual nature--they are real tigers and paper tigers at the same time. In past history, before they won state power and for some time afterwards, the slave-owning class, the feudal landlord class and the bourgeoisie were vigorous, revolutionary and progressive; they were real tigers. But with the lapse of time, because their opposites--the slave class, the peasant class and the proletariat--grew in strength step by step, struggled against them more and more fiercely, these ruling classes changed step by step into the reverse, changed into reactionaries, changed into backward people, changed into paper tigers. And eventually they were overthrown, or will be overthrown, by the people. The reactionary, backward, decaying classes retained this dual nature even in their last life-and-death struggles against the people. On the one hand, they were real tigers; they devoured people, devoured people by the millions and tens of millions. The cause of the people's struggle went through a period of difficulties and hardships, and along the path there were many twists and turns. To destroy the rule of imperialism, feudalism and bureaucrat-capitalism in China took the Chinese people more than a hundred years and cost them tens of millions of lives before the victory in 1949. Look! Were these not living tigers, iron tigers, real tigers? But in the end they changed into paper tigers, dead tigers, bean-curd tigers. These are historical facts. Have people not seen or heard about these facts? There have indeed been thousands and tens of thousands of them! Thousands and tens of thousands! Hence, imperialism and all reactionaries, looked at in essence, from a long-term point of view, from a strategic point of view, must be seen for what they are--paper tigers. On this we should build our strategic thinking. On the other hand, they are also living tigers, iron tigers, real tigers which can devour people. On this we should build our tactical thinking.

Speech at the Wuchang Meeting of the Political Bureau of the Central Committee of the Communist Party of China (December 1, 1958), quoted in the explanatory note to "Talk with the American Correspondent Anna Louise Strong", Selected Works, Vol. IV, pp. 98-99.

I have said that all the reputedly powerful reactionaries are merely paper tigers. The reason is that they are divorced from the people. Look! Was not Hitler a paper tiger? Was Hitler not overthrown? I also said that the tsar of Russia, the emperor of China and Japanese imperialism were all paper tigers. As we know, they were all overthrown. U.S. imperialism has not yet been overthrown and it has the atom bomb. I believe it also will be overthrown. It, too, is a paper tiger.

Speech at the Moscow Meeting of Communist and Workers' Parties (November 18, 1957).

"Lifting a rock only to drop it on one's own feet" is a Chinese folk saying to describe the behaviour of certain fools. The reactionaries in all countries are fools of this kind. In the final analysis, their persecution of the revolutionary people only serves to accelerate the people's revolutions on a broader and more intense scale. Did not the persecution of the revolutionary people by the tsar of Russia and by Chiang Kai-shek perform this function in the Great Russian and Chinese revolutions?

"Speech at the Meeting of the Supreme Soviet of the U.S.S.R. in Celebration of the 40th Anniversary of the Great October Socialist Revolution" (November 6, 1957).

U.S. imperialism invaded China's territory of Taiwan and has occupied it for the past nine years. A short while ago it sent its armed forces to invade and occupy Lebanon. The United States has set up hundreds of military bases in many countries all over the world. China's territory of Taiwan, Lebanon and all military bases of the United States on foreign soil are so many nooses round the neck of U.S. imperialism. The nooses have been fashioned by the Americans themselves and by nobody else, and it is they themselves who have put these nooses round their own necks, handing the ends of the ropes to the Chinese people, the peoples of the Arab countries and all the peoples of the world who love peace and oppose aggression. The longer the U.S. aggressors remain in those places, the tighter the nooses round their necks will become.

Speech at the Supreme State Conference (September 8, 1958).

Imperialism will not last long because it always does evil things. It persists in grooming and supporting reactionaries in all countries who are against the people, it has forcibly seized many colonies and semi-colonies and many military bases, and it threatens the peace with atomic war. Thus, forced by imperialism to do so, more than 90 per cent of the people of the world are rising or will rise up in struggle against it. Yet imperialism is still alive, still running amuck in Asia, Africa and Latin America. In the West imperialism is still oppressing the people at home. This situation must change. It is the task of the people of the whole world to put an end to the aggression and oppression perpetrated by imperialism, and chiefly by U.S. imperialism.

Interview with a Hsinhua News Agency correspondent (September 29, 1958).

Riding roughshod everywhere, U.S. imperialism has made itself the enemy of the people of the world and has increasingly isolated itself. Those who refuse to be enslaved will never be cowed by the atom bombs and hydrogen bombs in the hands of the U.S. imperialists. The raging tide of the people of the world against the U.S. aggressors is irresistible. Their struggle against U.S. imperialism and its lackeys will assuredly win still greater victories.

"Statement Supporting the Panamanian People's Just Patriotic Struggle Against U.S. Imperialism" (January 12, 1964), People of the World, Unite and Defeat the U.S. Aggressors and All Their Lackeys, 2nd ed., pp. 9-10.
If the U.S. monopoly capitalist groups persist in pushing their policies of aggression and war, the day is bound to come when they will be hung by the people of the whole world. The same fate awaits the accomplices of the United States.

Speech at the Supreme State Conference (September 8, 1958).

Over a long period we have developed this concept for the struggle against the enemy: strategically we should despise all our enemies, but tactically we should take them all seriously. This also means that we must despise the enemy with respect to the whole, but that we must take him seriously with respect to each and every concrete question. If we do not despise the enemy with respect to the whole, we shall be committing the error of opportunism. Marx and Engel were only two individuals, and yet in those early days they already declared that capitalism would be overthrown throughout the world. But in dealing with concrete problems and particular enemies we shall be committing the error of adventurism unless we take them seriously. In war, battles can only be fought one by one and the enemy forces can only be destroyed one by one. Factories can only be built one by one. The peasants can only plough the land plot by plot. The same is even true of eating a meal. Strategically, we take the eating of a meal lightly-- we know we can finish it. But actually we eat it mouthful by mouthful. It is impossible to swallow an entire banquet in one gulp. This is known as a piecemeal solution. In military parlance, it is called wiping out the enemy forces one by one.

Speech at the Moscow Meeting of Communist and Workers' Parties (November 18, 1957).

It is my opinion that the international situation has now reached a new turning point. There are two winds in the world today, the East Wind and the West Wind. There is a Chinese saying, "Either the East Wind prevails over the West Wind or the West Wind prevails over the East Wind." I believe it is characteristic of the situation today that the East Wind is prevailing over the West Wind. That is to say, the forces of socialism have become overwhelmingly superior to the forces of imperialism.

Ibid.

7. DARE TO STRUGGLE AND DARE TO WIN

People of the world, unite and defeat the U.S. aggressors and all their running dogs! People of the world, be courageous, dare to fight, defy difficulties and advance wave upon wave. Then the whole world will belong to the people. Monsters of all kinds shall be destroyed.

"Statement Supporting the People of the Congo (L.) Against U.S. Aggression" (November 28, 1964), People of the World, Unite and Defeat the U.S. Aggressors and All Their Lackeys, 2nd ed., p. 14.

The Communist Party of China, having made a clear-headed appraisal of the international and domestic situation on the basis of the science of Marxism-Leninism, recognized that all attacks by the reactionaries at home and abroad had to be defeated and could be defeated. When dark clouds appeared in the sky, we pointed out that they were only temporary, that the darkness would soon pass and the sun break through.

"The Present Situation and Our Tasks" (December 25, 1947), Selected Military Writings, 2nd ed., p. 347.

Historically, all reactionary forces on the verge of extinction invariably conduct a last desperate struggle against the revolutionary forces, and some revolutionaries are apt to be deluded for a time by this phenomenon of outward strength but inner weakness failing to grasp the essential fact that the enemy is nearing extinction while they themselves are approaching victory.

"The Turning Point in World War II" (October 12, 1942), Selected Works, Vol. III, p. 103.

If they [the Kuomintang] fight, we will wipe them out completely. This is the way things are: if they attack and we wipe them out, they will have that satisfaction; wipe out some, some satisfaction; wipe out more, more satisfaction; wipe out the whole lot, complete satisfaction. China's problems are complicated, and our brains must also be a little complicated. If they start fighting, we fight back--fight to win peace.
"On the Chungking Negotiations" (October 17, 1945), Selected Works, Vol. IV, p. 56.

If anyone attacks us and if the conditions are favourable for battle, we will certainly act in self-defence to wipe him out resolutely, thoroughly, wholly and completely (we do not strike rashly, but when we do strike, we must win). We must never be cowed by the bluster of reactionaries.

"On Peace Negotiations with the Kuomintang--Circular of the Central Committee of the Communist Party of China" (August 26, 1945), Selected Works, Vol. IV, p. 49

As far as our own desire is concerned, we don't want to fight even for a single day. But if circumstances force us to fight, we can fight to the finish.

"Talk with the American Correspondent Anna Louise Strong" (August 1946), Selected Works, Vol. IV, p. 97.

We are for peace. But so long as U.S. imperialism refuses to give up its arrogant and unreasonable demands and its scheme to extend aggression, the only course for the Chinese people is to remain determined to go on fighting side by side with the Korean people. Not that we are warlike. We are willing to stop the war at once and leave the remaining questions for later settlement. But U.S. imperialism is not willing to do so. All right then, let the fighting go on. However many years U.S. imperialism wants to fight, we are ready to fight right up to the moment when it is willing to stop, right up to the moment of complete victory for the Chinese and Korean peoples.

Speech at the Fourth Session of the First National Committee of the Chinese People's Political Consultative Conference (February 7, 1953).

We should rid our ranks of all impotent thinking. All views that overestimate the strength of the enemy and underestimate the strength of the people are wrong.

"The Present Situation and Our Tasks" (December 25, 1947), Selected Works, Vol. IV, p. 173.
The oppressed peoples and nations must not pin their hopes for liberation on the "sensibleness" of imperialism and its lackeys. They will only triumph by strengthening their unity and persevering in their struggle.

"Statement Opposing Aggression Against Southern Vietnam and Slaughter of Its People by the U.S.-Ngo Dinh Diem Clique" (August 29, 1963), People of the World, Unite and Defeat the U.S. Aggressors and All Their Lackeys, 2nd ed., p. 6.

No matter when this countrywide civil war breaks out, we must be well prepared. If it comes early, say, tomorrow morning, we should also be prepared. That is point one. In the present international and domestic situation it is possible that for a time the civil war may be kept restricted in scale and localized. That is point two. Point one is what we should prepare for; point two is what has existed for a long time. In short, we must be prepared. Being prepared, we shall be able to deal properly with all kinds of complicated situations.

"The Situation and Our Policy After the Victory in the War of Resistance Against Japan" (August 13, 1945), Selected Works, Vol. IV, p. 22.

8. PEOPLE'S WAR

The revolutionary war is a war of the masses; it can be waged only by mobilizing the masses and relying on them.

"Be Concerned with the Well-Being of the Masses, Pay Attention to Methods of Work" (January 27, 1934), Selected Works, Vol. I. p. 147.

What is a true bastion of iron? It is the masses, the millions upon millions of people who genuinely and sincerely support the revolution. That is the real iron bastion which it is impossible, and absolutely impossible, for any force on earth to smash. The counter-revolution cannot smash us; on the contrary, we shall smash it. Rallying millions upon millions of people round the revolutionary government and expanding our revolutionary war, we shall wipe out all counter-revolution and take over the whole of China.

Ibid. p. 150.

The richest source of power to wage war lies in the masses of the people. It is mainly because of the unorganized state of the Chinese masses that Japan dares to bully us. When this defect is remedied, then the Japanese aggressor, like a mad bull crashing into a ring of flames, will be surrounded by hundreds of millions of our people standing upright, the mere sound of their voices will strike terror into him, and he will be burned to death.

"On Protracted War" (May 1938), Selected Works, Vol. II, p. 186.

The imperialists are bullying us in such a way that we will have to deal with them seriously. Not only must we have a powerful regular army, we must also organize contingents of the people's militia on a big scale. This will make it difficult for the imperialists to move a single inch in our country in the event of invasion.

Interview with a Hsinhua News Agency correspondent (September 29, 1958).

Considering the revolutionary war as a whole, the operations of the people's guerrillas and those of the main forces of the Red Army complement each other like a man's right arm and left arm, and if we had only the main forces of the Red Army without the people's guerrillas, we would be like a warrior with only one arm. In concrete terms, and especially with regard to military operations, when we talk of the people in the base area as a factor, we mean that we have an armed people. That is the main reason why the enemy is afraid to approach our base area.

"Problems of Strategy in China's Revolutionary War" (December 1936), Selected Works, Vol. I, p. 238.

Unquestionably, victory or defeat in war is determined mainly by the military, political, economic and natural conditions on both sides, but not by these alone. It is also determined by each side's subjective ability in directing the war. In his endeavour to win a war, a military strategist cannot overstep the limitations imposed by the material conditions; within these limitations, however, he can and must strive for victory. The stage of action for a military strategist is built upon objective material conditions, but on that stage he can direct the performance of many a drama, full of sound and colour, power and grandeur.

Ibid. pp. 190-91.

The object of war is specifically "to preserve oneself and destroy the enemy" (to destroy the enemy means to disarm him or "deprive him of the power to resist", and does not mean to destroy every member of his forces physically). In ancient warfare, the spear and the shield were used, the spear to attack and destroy the enemy, and the shield to defend and preserve oneself. To the present day, all weapons are still an extension of the spear and the shield. The bomber, the machine-gun, the long-range gun and poison gas are developments of the spear, while the air-raid shelter, the steel helmet, the concrete fortification and the gas mask are developments of the shield. The tank is a new weapon combining the functions of both spear and shield. Attack is the chief means of destroying the enemy, but defence cannot be dispensed with. In attack the immediate object is to destroy the enemy, but at the same time it is self-preservation, because if the enemy is not destroyed, you will be destroyed. In defence the immediate object is to preserve yourself, but at the same time defence is a means of supplementing attack or preparing to go over to the attack. Retreat is in the category of defence and is a continuation of defence, while pursuit is a continuation of attack. It should be pointed out that destruction of the enemy is the primary object of war and self-preservation the secondary, because only by destroying the enemy in large numbers can one effectively preserve oneself. Therefore attack, the chief means of destroying the enemy, is primary, while defence, a supplementary means of destroying the enemy and a means of self-preservation, is secondary. In actual warfare the chief role is played by defence much of the time and by attack for the rest of the time, but if war is taken as a whole, attack remains primary.

"On Protracted War" (May 1938). Selected Works, Vol. II, p. 156.

All the guiding principles of military operations grow out of the one basic principle: to strive to the utmost to preserve one's own strength and destroy that of the enemy. How then do we justify the encouragement of heroic sacrifice in war? Every war exacts a price, sometimes an extremely high one. Is this not in contradiction with "preserving oneself"? In fact, there is no contradiction at all; to put it more exactly, sacrifice and self-preservation are both opposite and complementary to each other. For such sacrifice is essential not only for destroying the enemy but also for preserving oneself--partial and temporary "non-preservation" (sacrifice, or paying the price) is necessary for the sake of general and permanent preservation. From this basic principle stems the series of principles guiding military operations, all of which--from the principles of shooting (taking cover to preserve oneself, and making full use of fire-power to destroy the enemy) to the principles of strategy--are permeated with the spirit of this basic principle. All technical principles and all principles concerning tactics, campaigns and strategy represent applications of this basic principle. The principle of preserving oneself and destroying the enemy is the basis of all military principles.

"Problems of Strategy in Guerrilla War Against Japan" (May 1938), Selected Works, Vol. II, pp. 81-82.

Our principles of operation are:
(1) Attack dispersed, isolated enemy forces first; attack concentrated, strong enemy forces later.
(2) Take small and medium cities and extensive rural areas first; take big cities later.

(3) Make wiping out the enemy's effective strength our main objective; do not make holding or seizing a city or place our main objective. Holding or seizing a city or place is the outcome of wiping out the enemy's effective strength, and often a city or place can be held or seized for good only after it has changed hands a number of times.

(4) In every battle, concentrate an absolutely superior force (two, three, four and sometimes even five or six times the enemy's strength), encircle the enemy forces completely, strive to wipe them out thoroughly and do not let any escape from the net. In special circumstances, use the method of dealing the enemy crushing blows, that is, concentrate all our strength to make a frontal attack and an attack on one or both of his flanks, with the aim of wiping out one part and routing another so that our army can swiftly move its troops to smash other enemy forces. Strive to avoid battles of attrition in which we lose more than we gain or only break even. In this way, although inferior as a whole (in terms of numbers), we shall be absolutely superior in every part and every specific campaign, and this ensures victory in the campaign. As time goes on, we shall become superior as a whole and eventually wipe out all the enemy.

(5) Fight no battle unprepared, fight no battle you are not sure of winning; make every effort to be well prepared for each battle, make every effort to ensure victory in the given set of conditions as between the enemy and ourselves.

(6) Give full play to our style of fighting--courage in battle, no fear of sacrifice, no fear of fatigue, and continuous fighting (that is, fighting successive battles in a short time without rest).

(7) Strive to wipe out the enemy when he is on the move. At the same time, pay attention to the tactics of positional attack and capture enemy fortified points and cities.

(8) With regard to attacking cities, resolutely seize all enemy fortified points and cities which are weakly defended. At opportune moments, seize all enemy fortified points and cities defended with moderate strength, provided circumstances permit. As for all strongly defended enemy fortified points and cities, wait till conditions are ripe and then take them.

(9) Replenish our strength with all the arms and most of the personnel captured from the enemy. Our army's main sources of manpower and materiel are at the front.

(10) Make good use of the intervals between campaigns to rest, train and consolidate our troops. Periods of rest, training and consolidation should not in general be very long, and the enemy should so far as possible be permitted no breathing space.

These are the main methods the People's Liberation Army has employed in defeating Chiang Kai-shek. They are the result of the tempering of the People's Liberation Army in long years of fighting against domestic and foreign enemies and are completely suited to our present situation...our strategy and tactics are based on a people's war; no army opposed to the people can use our strategy and tactics.

"The Present Situation and Our Tasks" (December 25, 1947), Selected Military Writings, 2nd ed., pp. 349-50.

Without preparedness superiority is not real superiority and there can be no initiative either. Having grasped this point, a force which is inferior but prepared, can often defeat a superior enemy by surprise attack.

"On Protracted War" (May 1938), Selected Works, Vol. II, pp. 165-66.

9. THE PEOPLE'S ARMY

Without a people's army the people have nothing.

"On Coalition Government" (April 24, 1945), Selected Works, Vol. III, pp. 296-97.

This army is powerful because all its members have a conscious discipline; they have come together and they fight not for the private interests of a few individuals or a narrow clique, but for the interests of the broad masses and of the whole nation. The sole purpose of this army is to stand firmly with the Chinese people and to serve them whole-heartedly.

Ibid. p. 264.

The Chinese Red Army is an armed body for carrying out the political tasks of the revolution. Especially at present, the Red Army should certainly not confine itself to fighting; besides fighting to destroy the enemy's military strength, it should shoulder such important tasks as doing propaganda among the masses, organizing the masses, arming them, helping them to establish revolutionary political power and setting up Party organizations. The Red Army fights not merely for the sake of fighting but in order to conduct propaganda among the masses, organize them, arm them, and help them to establish revolutionary political power. Without these objectives, fighting loses its meaning and the Red Army loses the reason for its existence.

"On Correcting Mistaken Ideas in the Party" (December 1929), Selected Works, Vol. I, p. 106.

The People's Liberation Army is always a fighting force. Even after countrywide victory, our army will remain a fighting force during the historical period in which classes have not been abolished in our country and the imperialist system still exists in the world. On this point there should be no misunderstanding or wavering.

"Report to the Second Plenary Session of the Seventh Central Committee of the Communist Party of China" (March 5, 1949), Selected Works, Vol. IV, p. 362.

We have an army for fighting as well as an army for labour. For fighting we have the Eighth Route and New Fourth Armies but even they do a dual job, warfare and production. With these two kinds of armies, and with a fighting army skilled in these two tasks and in mass work, we can overcome our difficulties and defeat Japanese imperialism.

"Get Organized!" (November 29), Selected Works, Vol. III, p. 153.

Our national defence will be consolidated and no imperialist will be allowed to invade our territory again. Our people's armed forces must be maintained and developed with the brave and steeled People's Liberation Army as their foundation. We will have not only a powerful army but also a powerful air force and a powerful navy.

Opening address at the First Plenary Session of the Chinese People's Political Consultative Conference (September 21, 1949).

Our principle is that the Party commands the gun, and the gun must never be allowed to command the Party.

"Problems of War and Strategy" (November 6, 1938), Selected Works, Vol. II, p. 224.

All our officers and fighters must always bear in mind that we are the great People's Liberation Army; we are the troops led by the great Communist Party of China. Provided we constantly observe the directives of the Party, we are sure to win.

"Manifesto of the Chinese People's Liberation Army" (October 1947), Selected Works, Vol. IV, p. 152.

10. LEADERSHIP OF PARTY COMMITTEES

The Party committee system is an important Party institution for ensuring collective leadership and preventing any individual from monopolizing the conduct of affairs. It has recently been found that in some (of course not all) leading bodies it is the habitual practice for one individual to monopolize the conduct of affairs and decide important problems. Solutions to important problems are decided not by Party committee meetings but by one individual, and membership in the Party committee has become nominal. Differences of opinion among committee members cannot be resolved and are left unresolved for a long time. Members of the Party committee maintain only formal, not real, unity among themselves. This situation must be changed. From now on, a sound system of Party committee meetings must be instituted in all leading bodies, from the regional bureaus of the Central Committee to the prefectural Party committees; from the Party committees of the fronts to the Party committees of brigades and military areas (sub-commissions of the Revolutionary Military Commission or leading groups); and the leading Party members' groups in government bodies, people's organizations the news agency and the newspaper offices. All the important problems (of course, not the unimportant, trivial problems, or problems whose solutions have already been decided after discussion at meetings and need only be carried out) must be submitted to the committee for discussion, and the committee members present should express their views fully and reach definite decisions which should then be carried out by the members concerned. Party committee meetings must be divided into two categories, standing committee meetings and plenary sessions, and the two should not be confused. Furthermore, we must take care that neither collective leadership nor personal responsibility is overemphasized to the neglect of the other. In the army, the person in command has the right to make emergency decisions during battle and when circumstances require.

"On Strengthening the Party Committee System" (September 20, 1948), Selected Works, Vol. IV, pp. 267-68.

The secretary of a Party committee must be good at being a "squad leader". A Party committee has ten to twenty members; it is like a squad in the army, and the secretary is like the "squad leader". It is indeed not easy to lead this squad well. Each regional bureau or sub-regional bureau of the Central Committee now leads a vast area and shoulders very heavy responsibilities. To lead means not only to decide general and specific policies but also to devise correct methods of work. Even with correct general and specific policies, troubles may still arise if methods of work are neglected. To fulfill its task of exercising leadership, a Party committee must rely on its "squad members" and enable them to play their parts to the full. To be a good "squad leader", the secretary should study hard and investigate thoroughly. A secretary or deputy secretary will find it difficult to direct his "squad" well if he does not take care to do propaganda and organizational work among his own "squad members", is not good at handling his relations with committee members or does not study how to run meetings successfully. If the "squad members" do not march in step, they can never expect to lead tens of millions of people in fighting and construction. Of course, the relation between the secretary and the committee members is one in which the minority must obey the majority, so it is different from the relation between a squad leader and his men. Here we speak only by way of analogy.

"Methods of Work of Party Committees" (March 13, 1949), Selected Works, Vol. IV, p. 377.

Place problems on the table. This should be done not only by the "squad leader" but by the committee members too. Do not talk behind people's backs. Whenever problems arise, call a meeting, place the problems on the table for discussion, take some decisions and the problems will be solved. If problems exist and are not placed on the table, they will remain unsolved for a long time and even drag on for years. The "squad leader" and the committee members should show understanding in their relations with each other. Nothing is more important than mutual understanding, support and friendship between the secretary and the committee members, between the Central Committee and its regional bureaus and between the regional bureaus and the area Party committees.

Ibid. pp. 377-78.

"Exchange information." This means that members of a Party committee should keep each other informed and exchange views on matters that have come to their attention. This is of great importance in achieving a common language. Some fail to do so and, like the people described by Lao Tzu, "do not visit each other all their lives, though the crowing of their cocks and the barking of their dogs are within hearing of each other". The result is that they lack a common language.

Ibid. p. 378.

Ask your subordinates about matters you don't understand or don't know, and do not lightly express your approval or disapproval.... We should never pretend to know what we don't know, we should "not feel ashamed to ask and learn from people below" and we should listen carefully to the views of the cadres at the lower levels. Be a pupil before you become a teacher; learn from the cadres at the lower levels before you issue orders. What the cadres at the lower levels say may or may not be correct, after hearing it, we must analyse it. We must heed the correct views and act upon them. Listen also to the mistaken views from below, it is wrong not to listen to them at all. Such views, however, are not to be acted upon but to be criticized.

Ibid. pp. 378-79

Learn to "play the piano". In playing the piano all ten fingers are in motion; it won't do to move some fingers only and not others. But if all ten fingers press down at once, there is no melody. To produce good music, the ten fingers should move rhythmically and in co-ordination. A Party committee should keep a firm grasp on its central task and at the same time, around the central task, it should unfold the work in other fields. At present, we have to take care of many fields; we must look after the work in all the areas, armed units and departments, and not give all our attention to a few problems, to the exclusion of others. Wherever there is a problem, we must put our finger on it, and this is a method we must master. Some play the piano well and some badly, and there is a great difference in the melodies they produce. Members of Party committees must learn to "play the piano" well.

Ibid. p. 379.

"Grasp firmly." That is to say, the Party committee must not merely "grasp", but must "grasp firmly", its main tasks. One can get a grip on something only when it is grasped firmly, without the slightest slackening. Not to grasp firmly is not to grasp at all. Naturally, one cannot get a grip on something with an open hand. When the hand is clenched as if grasping something but is not clenched tightly, there is still no grip. Some of our comrades do grasp the main tasks, but their grasp is not firm and so they cannot make a success of their work. It will not do to have no grasp at all, nor will it do if the grasp is not firm.

Ibid.

"Have a head for figures." That is to say, we must attend to the quantitative aspect of a situation or problem and make a basic quantitative analysis. Every quality manifests itself in a certain quantity, and without quantity there can be no quality. To this day many of our comrades still do not understand that they must attend to the quantitative aspect of things--the basic statistics, the main percentages and the quantitative limits that determine the qualities of things. They have no "figures" in their heads and as a result cannot help making mistakes.

Ibid. pp. 379-80.

"Notice to Reassure the Public." Notice of meetings should be given beforehand; this is like issuing a "Notice to Reassure the Public", so that everybody will know what is going to be discussed and what problems are to be solved and can make timely preparations. In some places, meetings of cadres are called without first preparing reports and draft resolutions, and only when people have arrived for the meeting are makeshifts improvised; this is just like the saying, "Troops and horses have arrived, but food and fodder are not ready", and that is no good. Don't call a meeting in a hurry if the preparations are not completed.

Ibid. p. 380.

"Fewer and better troops and simpler administration." Talks, speeches, articles and resolutions should all be concise and to the point. Meetings also should not go on too long.
Ibid.

Pay attention to uniting and working with comrades who differ with you. This should be borne in mind both in the localities and in the army. It also applies to relations with people outside the Party. We have come together from every corner of the country and should be good at uniting in our work not only with comrades who hold the same views as we but also with those who hold different views.

Ibid.

Guard against arrogance. For anyone in a leading position, this is a matter of principle and an important condition for maintaining unity. Even those who have made no serious mistakes and have achieved very great success in their work should not be arrogant.

Ibid.

Draw two lines of distinction. First, between revolution and counter-revolution; between Yenan and Sian. [1] Some do not understand that they must draw this line of distinction. For example, when they combat bureaucracy, they speak of Yenan as though "nothing is right" there and fail to make a comparison and distinguish between the bureaucracy in Yenan and the bureaucracy in Sian. This is fundamentally wrong. Secondly, within the revolutionary ranks, it is necessary to make a clear distinction between right and wrong, between achievements and shortcomings and to make clear which of the two is primary and which secondary. For instance, do the achievements amount to 30 per cent or to 70 per cent of the whole? It will not do either to understate or to overstate. We must have a fundamental evaluation of a person's work and establish whether his achievements amount to 30 per cent and his mistakes to 70 per cent, or vice versa. If his achievements amount to 70 per cent of the whole, then his work should in the main be approved. It would be entirely wrong to describe work in which the achievements are primary as work in which the mistakes are primary. In our approach to problems we must not forget to draw these two lines of distinction, between revolution and counter-revolution and between achievements and shortcomings. We shall be able to handle things well if we bear these two distinctions in mind; otherwise we shall confuse the nature of the problems. To draw these distinctions well, careful study and analysis are of course necessary. Our attitude towards every person and every matter should be one of analysis and study.

Ibid. p. 381.

In the sphere of organization, ensure democracy under centralized guidance. It should be done on the following lines:

(1) The leading bodies of the Party must give a correct line of guidance and find solutions when problems arise, in order to establish themselves as centres of leadership.
(2) The higher bodies must be familiar with the situation in the lower bodies and with the life of the masses so as to have an objective basis for correct guidance.
(3) No Party organization at any level should make casual decisions in solving problems. Once a decision is reached, it must be firmly carried out.
(4) All decisions of any importance made by the Party's higher bodies must be promptly transmitted to the lower bodies and the Party rank and file.
(5) The lower bodies of the Party and the Party rank and file must discuss the higher bodies' directives in detail in order to understand their meaning thoroughly and decide on the methods of carrying them out.

"On Correcting Mistaken Ideas in the Party" (December 1929), Selected Works, Vol. I, p. 109.

Note:
1. Yenan was the headquarters of the Central Committee of the Communist Party of China from January 1937 to March 1947; Sian was the centre of the reactionary rule of the Kuomintang in northwestern China. Comrade Mao Tse-tung cited the two cities as symbols of revolution and counterrevolution.

11. THE MASS LINE

The people, and the people alone, are the motive force in the making of world history.

"On Coalition Government" (April 24, 1945), Selected Works, Vol. III, p. 257.

The masses are the real heroes, while we ourselves are often childish and ignorant, and without this understanding it is impossible to acquire even the most rudimentary knowledge.

"Preface and Postscript to Rural Surveys" (March and April 1941), Selected Works, Vol. III, p. 12.

The masses have boundless creative power. They can organize themselves and concentrate on places and branches of work where they can give full play to their energy; they can concentrate on production in breadth and depth and create more and more undertakings for their own well-being.

Introductory note to "Surplus Labour Has Found a Way Out" (1955), The Socialist Upsurge in China's Countryside, Chinese ed., Vol. II.

The present upsurge of the peasant movement is a colossal event. In a very short time, in China's central, southern and northern provinces, several hundred million peasants will rise like a mighty storm, like a hurricane, a force so swift and violent that no power, however great, will be able to hold it back. They will smash all the trammels that bind them and rush forward along the road to liberation. They will sweep all the imperialists, warlords, corrupt officials, local tyrants and evil gentry into their graves. Every revolutionary party and every revolutionary comrade will be put to the test, to be accepted or rejected as they decide. There are three alternatives: To march at their head and lead them; to trail behind them, gesticulating and criticizing; or to stand in their way and oppose them. Every Chinese is free to choose, but events will force you to make the choice quickly.

"Report on an Investigation of the Peasant Movement in Hunan" (March 1927), Selected Works, Vol. I, pp. 23-24.

The high tide of social transformation in the countryside, the high tide of co-operation, has already reached some places and will soon sweep over the whole country. It is a vast socialist revolutionary movement involving a rural population of more than 100 million, and it has extremely great and worldwide significance. We should give this movement active, enthusiastic and systematic leadership, and not drag it back by one means or another. Some errors are unavoidable in the process; this is understandable, and they will not be hard to correct. Shortcomings or mistakes found among the cadres and the peasants can be remedied or overcome provided we give them positive help.

On the Question of Agricultural Co-operation (July 31, 1955), 3rd ed., p. 1.

The masses have a potentially inexhaustible enthusiasm for socialism. Those who can only follow the old routine in a revolutionary period are utterly incapable of seeing this enthusiasm. They are blind and all is dark ahead of them. At times they go so far as to confound right and wrong and turn things upside down. Haven't we come across enough persons of this type? Those who simply follow the old routine invariably underestimate the people's enthusiasm. Let something new appear and they always disapprove and rush to oppose it. Afterwards, they have to admit defeat and do a little self-criticism. But the next time something new appears, they go through the same process all over again. This is their pattern of behaviour in regard to anything and everything new. Such people are always passive, always fail to move forward at the critical moment, and always have to be given a shove in the back before they move a step.

Introductory note to "This Township Went Co-operative in Two Years" (1955), The Socialist Upsurge in China's Countryside, Chinese ed., Vol. II.

For over twenty years our Party has carried on mass work every day, and for the past dozen years it has talked about the mass line every day. We have always maintained that the revolution must rely on the masses of the people, on everybody's taking a hand, and have opposed relying merely on a few persons issuing orders. The mass line, however, is still not being thoroughly carried out in the work of some comrades; they still rely solely on a handful of people working in solitude. One reason is that, whatever they do, they are always reluctant to explain it to the people they lead and that they do not understand why or how to give play to the initiative and creative energy of those they lead. Subjectively, they too want everyone to take a hand in the work, but they do not let other people know what is to be done or how to do it. That being the case, how can everyone be expected to get moving and how can anything be done well? To solve this problem the basic thing is, of course, to carry out ideological education on the mass line, but at the same time we must teach these comrades many concrete methods of work.

"A Talk to the Editorial Staff of the Shansi-Suiyuan Daily" (April 2, 1948), Selected Works, Vol. IV, pp. 241-42.

Twenty-four years of experience tell us that the right task, policy and style of work invariably conform with the demands of the masses at a given time and place and invariably strengthen our ties with the masses, and the wrong task, policy and style of work invariably disagree with the demands of the masses at a given time and place and invariably alienate us from the masses. The reason why such evils as dogmatism, empiricism, commandism, tailism, sectarianism, bureaucracy and an arrogant attitude in work are definitely harmful and intolerable, and why anyone suffering from these maladies must overcome them, is that they alienate us from the masses.

"On Coalition Government" (April 24, 1945), Selected Works, Vol. III, p. 315.

To link oneself with the masses, one must act in accordance with the needs and wishes of the masses. All work done for the masses must start from their needs and not from the desire of any individual, however well intentioned. It often happens that objectively the masses need a certain change, but subjectively they are not yet conscious of the need, not yet willing or determined to make the change. In such cases, we should wait patiently. We should not make the change until, through our work, most of the masses have become conscious of the need and are willing and determined to carry it out. Otherwise we shall isolate ourselves from the masses. Unless they are conscious and willing, any kind of work that requires their participation will turn out to be a mere formality and will fail. There are two principles here: one is the actual needs of the masses rather than what we fancy they need, and the other is the wishes of the masses, who must make up their own minds instead of our making up their minds for them.

"The United Front in Cultural Work" (October 30, 1944), Selected Works, Vol. III, pp. 236-37.

Our congress should call upon the whole Party to be vigilant and to see that no comrade at any post is divorced from the masses. It should teach every comrade to love the people and listen attentively to the voice of the masses; to identify himself with the masses wherever he goes and, instead of standing above them, to immerse himself among them; and, according to their present level, to awaken them or raise their political consciousness and help them gradually to organize themselves voluntarily and to set going all essential struggles permitted by the internal and external circumstances of the given time and place.

"On Coalition Government" (April 24, 1945), Selected Works, Vol. III, pp. 315-16.

If we tried to go on the offensive when the masses are not yet awakened, that would be adventurism. If we insisted on leading the masses to do anything against their will, we would certainly fail. If we did not advance when the masses demand advance--that would be Right opportunism.

"A Talk to the Editorial Staff of the Shansi-Suiyuan Daily" (April 2, 1948), Selected Works, Vol. IV, p. 243.

Commandism is wrong in any type of work, because in overstepping the level of political consciousness of the masses and violating the principle of voluntary mass action it reflects the disease of impetuosity. Our comrades must not assume that everything they themselves understand is understood by the masses. Whether the masses understand it and are ready to take action can be discovered only by going into their midst and making investigations. If we do so, we can avoid commandism. Tailism in any type of work is also wrong, because in falling below the level of political consciousness of the masses and violating the principle of leading the masses forward it reflects the disease of dilatoriness. Our comrades must not assume that the masses have no understanding of what they themselves do not yet understand. It often happens that the masses outstrip us and are eager to advance a step and that nevertheless our comrades fail to act as leaders of the masses and tail behind certain backward elements, reflecting their views and, moreover, mistaking them for those of the broad masses.

"On Coalition Government" (April 24, 1945), Selected Works, Vol. III, p. 316.

Take the ideas of the masses and concentrate them, then go to the masses, persevere in the ideas and carry them through, so as to form correct ideas of leadership--such is the basic method of leadership.

"Some Questions Concerning Methods of Leadership" (June 1, 1943), Selected Works, Vol. III, p. 120.

In all the practical work of our Party, all correct leadership is necessarily "from the masses, to the masses". This means: take the ideas of the masses (scattered and unsystematic ideas) and concentrate them (through study turn them into concentrated and systematic ideas), then go to the masses and propagate and explain these ideas until the masses embrace them as their own, hold fast to them and translate them into action, and test the correctness of these ideas in such action. Then once again concentrate ideas from the masses and once again go to the masses so that the ideas are persevered in and carried through; and so on, over and over again in an endless spiral, with the ideas becoming more correct, more vital and richer each time. Such is the Marxist theory of knowledge.

Ibid. p. 119.

We should go to the masses and learn from them, synthesize their experience into better, articulated principles and methods, then do propaganda among the masses, and call upon them to put these principles and methods into practice so as to solve their problems and help them achieve liberation and happiness.
"Get Organized!" (November 29, 1943), Selected Works, Vol. III, p. 158.

There are people in our leading organs in some places who think that it is enough for the leaders alone to know the Party's policies and that there is no need to let the masses know them. This is one of the basic reasons why some of our work cannot be done well.

"A Talk to the Editorial Staff of the Shansi-Suiyuan Daily" (April 2, 1948), Selected Works, Vol. IV, p. 241.

In all mass movements we must make a basic investigation and analysis of the number of active supporters, opponents and neutrals and must not decide problems subjectively and without basis.

"Methods of Work of Party Committees" (March 13, 1949), Selected Works, Vol. IV, p. 380.

The masses in any given place are generally composed of three parts, the relatively active, the intermediate and the relatively backward. The leaders must therefore be skilled in uniting the small number of active elements around the leadership and must rely on them to raise the level of the intermediate elements and to win over the backward elements.

"Some Questions Concerning Methods of Leadership" (June 1, 1943), Selected Works, Vol. III, p. 118.

To be good at translating the Party's policy into action of the masses, to be good at getting not only the leading cadres but also the broad masses to understand and master every movement and every struggle we launch--this is an art of Marxist-Leninist leadership. It is also the dividing line that determines whether or not we make mistakes in our work.

"A Talk to the Editorial Staff of the Shansi-Suiyuan Daily" (April 2, 1948), Selected Works, Vol. IV, pp 242-43.

However active the leading group may be, its activity will amount to fruitless effort by a handful of people unless combined with the activity of the masses. On the other hand, if the masses alone are active without a strong leading group to organize their activity properly, such activity cannot be sustained for long, or carried forward in the right direction, or raised to a high level.

"Some Questions Concerning Methods of Leadership" (June 1, 1943), Selected Works, Vol. III, p. 118.

Production by the masses, the interests of the masses, the experiences and feelings of the masses-- to these the leading cadres should pay constant attention.

Inscription for a production exhibition sponsored by organizations directly under the Central Committee of the Party and the General Headquarters of the Eighth Route Army, Liberation Daily of Yenan, November 24, 1943.

We should pay close attention to the well-being of the masses, from the problems of land and labour to those of fuel, rice, cooking oil and salt. All such problems concerning the well-being of the masses should be placed on our agenda. We should discuss them, adopt and carry out decisions and check up on the results. We should help the masses to realize that we represent their interests; that our lives are intimately bound up with theirs. We should help them to proceed from these things to an understanding of the higher tasks which we have put forward, the tasks of the revolutionary war, so that they will support the revolution and spread it throughout the country, respond to our political appeals and fight to the end for victory in the revolution.

"Be Concerned with the Well-Being of the Masses, Pay Attention to Methods of Work" (January 27, 1934), Selected Works, Vol. I, p. 149.

12. POLITICAL WORK

The system of Party representatives and of political departments, adopted for the first time in China, entirely changed the complexion of these armed forces. [1] The Red Army, which was founded in 1927, and the Eighth Route Army of today have inherited this system and developed it.

"Interview with the British Journalist James Bertram" (October 25, 1937), Selected Works, Vol. II, p. 54.

The People's Liberation Army has developed its vigorous revolutionary political work, which is an important factor in winning victory over the enemy, on the basis of a people's war and of the principles of unity between army and people, of unity between commanders and fighters and of disintegrating the enemy troops.

"The Present Situation and Our Tasks" (December 25, 1947), Selected Military Writings, 2nd ed., p. 350.

This army has built up a system of political work which is essential for the people's war and is aimed at promoting unity in its own ranks, unity with the friendly armies and unity with the people, and at disintegrating the enemy forces and ensuring victory in battle.

"On Coalition Government" (April 24, 1945), Selected Works, Vol. III, p. 265.

Political work is the life-blood of all economic work. This is particularly true at a time when the social and economic system is undergoing fundamental change.

Introductory note to "A Serious Lesson" (1955), The Socialist Upsurge in China's Countryside, Chinese ed., Vol. I.

"The Party branch is organized on a company basis"; this is an important reason why the Red Army has been able to carry on such arduous fighting without falling apart.

"The Struggle in the Chingkang Mountains" (November 25, 1928), Selected Works, Vol. I, p. 84.

The political work of the Eighth Route Army is guided by three basic principles. First, the principle of unity between officers and men, which means eradicating feudal practices in the army, prohibiting beating and abuse, building up a conscious discipline, and sharing weal and woe--as a result of which the entire army is closely united. Second, the principle of unity between the army and the people, which means maintaining a discipline that forbids the slightest violation of the people's interests, conducting propaganda among the masses, organizing and arming them, lightening their economic burdens and suppressing the traitors and collaborators who do harm to the army and the people--as a result of which the army is closely united with the people and welcomed everywhere. Third, the principle of disintegrating the enemy troops and giving lenient treatment to prisoners of war. Our victory depends not only upon our military operations but also upon the disintegration of the enemy troops.

"Interview with the British Journalist James Bertram" (October 25, 1937), Selected Works, Vol. II, p. 53.

Our troops must observe the correct principles that govern relations between the army and the people, between the army and the government, between the army and the Party, between officers and men, and between military work and political work, and relations among the cadres, and must never commit the errors of warlordism. Officers must cherish their men and must not be indifferent to their well-being or resort to corporal punishment; the army must cherish the people and never encroach upon their interests; the army must respect the government and the Party and never "assert independence".

"Get Organized!" (November 29, 1943), Selected Works, Vol. III, pp. 158-59.

Our policy towards prisoners captured from the Japanese, puppet or anti-Communist troops is to set them all free, except for those who have incurred the bitter hatred of the masses and must receive capital punishment and whose death sentence has been approved by the higher authorities. Among the prisoners, those who were coerced into joining the reactionary forces but who are more or less inclined towards the revolution should be won over in large numbers to work for our army. The rest should be released and, if they fight us and are captured again, should again be set free. We should not insult them, take away their personal effects or try to exact recantations from them, but without exception should treat them sincerely and kindly. This should be our policy, however reactionary they may be. It is a very effective way of isolating the camp of reaction.

"On Policy" (December 25, 1940), Selected Works, Vol. II, pp. 446-47.

Weapons are an important factor in war, but not the decisive factor; it is people, not things, who are decisive. The contest of strength is not only a contest of military and economic power, but also a contest of human power and morale. Military and economic power is necessarily wielded by people.

"On Protracted War" (May 1958), Selected Works, Vol. II, pp. 143-44.

The atom bomb is a paper tiger which the U.S. reactionaries use to scare people. It looks terrible, but in fact it isn't. Of course, the atom bomb is a weapon of mass slaughter, but the outcome of a war is decided by the people--not by one or two new types of weapon.

"Talk with the American Correspondent Anna Louise Strong" (August 1946), Selected Works, Vol. IV, p. 100.

Soldiers are the foundation of an army; unless they are imbued with a progressive political spirit, and unless such a spirit is fostered through progressive political work, it will be impossible to achieve genuine unity between officers and men, impossible to arouse their enthusiasm for the War of Resistance to the full, and impossible to provide an excellent basis for the most effective use of all our technical equipment and tactics.

"On Protracted War" (May 1938), Selected Works, Vol. II, p. 185.

The purely military viewpoint is very highly developed among a number of comrades in the Red Army. It manifests itself as follows:

1. These comrades regard military affairs and politics as opposed to each other and refuse to recognize that military affairs are only one means of accomplishing political tasks. Some even say, "If you are good militarily, naturally you are good politically; if you are not good militarily, you cannot be any good politically"--this is to go a step further and give military affairs a leading position over politics.

"On Correcting Mistaken Ideas in the Party" (December 1929), Selected Works, Vol. I, pp. 105-06.

Ideological education is the key link to be grasped in uniting the whole Party for great political struggles. Unless this is done, the Party cannot accomplish any of its political tasks.

"On Coalition Government" (April 24, 1945), Selected Works, Vol. III, p. 315.

Recently there has been a falling off in ideological and political work among students and intellectuals, and some unhealthy tendencies have appeared. Some people seem to think that there is no longer any need to concern oneself with politics or with the future of the motherland and the ideals of mankind. It seems as if Marxism was once all the rage but is currently not so much in fashion. To counter these tendencies, we must strengthen our ideological and political work. Both students and intellectuals should study hard. In addition to the study of their specialized subjects, they must make progress both ideologically and politically, which means that they should study Marxism, current events and politics. Not to have a correct political point of view is like having no soul. All departments and organizations should shoulder their responsibilities in ideological and political work. This applies to the Communist Party, the Youth League, government departments in charge of this work, and especially to heads of educational institutions and teachers.

On the Correct Handling of Contradictions Among the People (February 27, 1957); 1st pocket ed., pp. 43-44.

After receiving political education, the Red Army soldiers have all become class-conscious and learned the essentials of distributing land, setting up political power, arming the workers and peasants, etc., and they all know they are fighting for themselves, for the working class and the peasantry. Hence they can endure the hardships of the bitter struggle without complaint. Each company, battalion or regiment has its soldiers' committee which represents the interests of the soldiers and carries on political and mass work.

"The Struggle in the Chingkang Mountains" (November 25, 1928), Selected Works, Vol. I, p. 81.

The correct unfolding of the movement for pouring out grievances (the wrongs done to the labouring people by the old society and by the reactionaries) and the three check-ups (on class origin, performance of duty and will to fight) greatly heightened the political consciousness of commanders and fighters throughout the army in the fight for the emancipation of the exploited working masses, for nationwide land reform and for the destruction of the common enemy of the people, the Chiang Kai-shek bandit gang. It also greatly strengthened the firm unity of all commanders and fighters under the leadership of the Communist Party. On this basis, the army achieved greater purity in its ranks, strengthened discipline, unfolded a mass movement for training, and further developed its political, economic and military democracy in a completely well led and orderly way. Thus the army has become united as one man, with everybody contributing his ideas and his strength, an army fearless of sacrifice and capable of overcoming material difficulties, which displays mass heroism and daring in destroying the enemy. Such an army will be invincible.

"On the Great Victory in the Northwest and on the New Type of Ideological Education Movement in the Liberation Army" (March 7, 1948), Selected Military Writings, 2nd ed., pp. 358-59.

In the last few months almost all the People's Liberation Army has made use of the intervals between battles for large-scale training and consolidation. This has been carried out in a fully guided, orderly and democratic way. It has therefore aroused the revolutionary fervor of the great masses of commanders and fighters, enabled them clearly to comprehend the aim of the war, eliminated certain incorrect ideological tendencies and undesirable manifestations in the army, educated the cadres and fighters and greatly enhanced the combat effectiveness of the army. From now on, we must continue to carry on this new type of ideological education movement in the army, a movement which has a democratic and mass character.

"Speech at a Conference of Cadres in the Shansi-Suiyuan Liberated Area" (April 1, 1948), Selected Works, Vol. IV, p. 234.

The educational policy of the college [the Anti-Japanese Military and Political College] is to cultivate a firm and correct political orientation, an industrious and simple style of work, and flexible strategy and tactics. These are the three essentials in the making of an anti-Japanese revolutionary soldier. It is in accordance with these essentials that the staff teach and the students study.

To Be Attacked by the Enemy Is Not a Bad Thing but a Good Thing (May 26, 1939), 1st pocket ed., p. 3.

Our nation has always had a traditional style of hard struggle, which we should develop. What is more, the Communist Party has always advocated a firm and correct political orientation. This orientation is inseparable from a style of hard struggle. Without a firm and correct political orientation, it is impossible to promote a style of hard struggle. Without the style of hard struggle, it is impossible to maintain a firm and correct political orientation.

"Speech at the Yenan Rally in Celebration of International Labour Day" (May 1, 1939).

Be united, alert, earnest and lively.

Motto for the Anti-Japanese Military and Political College.

What really counts in the world is conscientiousness, and the Communist Party is most particular about being conscientious.

Talk at a meeting with Chinese students and trainees in Moscow (November 17, 1957).

Note:
1. This refers to the revolutionary armed forces organized jointly by the Chinese Communist Party and the Kuomintang in the years of their cooperation during the First Revolutionary Civil War Period (1924-27).-- Tr.

13. RELATIONS BETWEEN OFFICERS AND MEN

Our army has always had two policies. First, we must be ruthless to our enemies; we must overpower and annihilate them. Second, we must be kind to our own, to the people, to our comrades and to our superiors and subordinates, and unite with them.

Speech at the reception given by the Central Committee of the Party for model study delegates from the Rear Army Detachments (September 18, 1944).

We hail from all corners of the country and have joined together for a common revolutionary objective. Our cadres must show concern for every soldier, and all people in the revolutionary ranks must care for each other, must love and help each other.

"Serve the People" (September 8, 1944), Selected Works, Vol. III, pp. 227-28.

A movement to support the cadres and cherish the soldiers should be launched in every army unit, calling on the cadres to cherish the soldiers and the soldiers to support the cadres. They should speak up about each other's shortcomings and mistakes and quickly correct them. In this way they will be able to achieve a very good internal unity.

"The Tasks for 1945" (December 15, 1944)

Many people think that it is wrong methods that make for strained relations between officers and men and between the army and the people, but I always tell them that it is a question of basic attitude (or basic principle), of having respect for the soldiers and the people. It is from this attitude that the various policies, methods and forms ensue. If we depart from this attitude, then the policies, methods and forms will certainly be wrong, and the relations between officers and men and between the army and the people are bound to be unsatisfactory. Our three major principles for the army's political work are, first, unity between officers and men; second, unity between the army and the people; and third, the disintegration of the enemy forces. To apply these principles effectively, we must start with this basic attitude of respect for the soldiers and the people, and of respect for the human dignity of prisoners of war once they have laid down their arms. Those who take all this as a technical matter and not one of basic attitude are indeed wrong, and they should correct their view.

"On Protracted War" (May 1938), Selected Works, Vol. II, pp. 186-87.

Communists must use the democratic method of persuasion and education when working among the labouring people and must on no account resort to commandism or coercion. The Chinese Communist Party faithfully adheres to this Marxist-Leninist principle.

On the Correct Handling of Contradictions Among the People (February 27, 1957), 1st pocket ed., p. 15.

Our comrades must understand that ideological remolding involves long-term, patient and painstaking work, and they must not attempt to change people's ideology, which has been shaped over decades of life, by giving a few lectures or by holding a few meetings. Persuasion, not compulsion, is the only way to convince them. Compulsion will never result in convincing them. To try to convince them by force simply won't work. This kind of method is permissible in dealing with the enemy, but absolutely impermissible in dealing with comrades or friends.

Speech at the Chinese Communist Party's National Conference on Propaganda Work (March 12, 1957), 1st pocket ed., p. 23.

We must make a distinction between the enemy and ourselves, and we must not adopt an antagonistic stand towards comrades and treat them as we would the enemy. In speaking up, one must have an ardent desire to protect the cause of the people and raise their political consciousness, and there must be no ridiculing or attacking in one's approach.

Ibid. p. 20.

14. RELATIONS BETWEEN THE ARMY AND THE PEOPLE

The army must become one with the people so that they see it as their own army. Such an army will be invincible.

"On Protracted War" (May 1938), Selected Works, Vol. II, p. 186.

Every comrade must be helped to understand that as long as we rely on the people, believe firmly in the inexhaustible creative power of the masses and hence trust and identify ourselves with them, we can surmount any difficulty, and no enemy can crush us while we can crush any enemy.

"On Coalition Government" (April 24, 1945), Selected Works, Vol. III, p. 316.

Wherever our comrades go, they must build good relations with the masses, be concerned for them and help them overcome their difficulties. We must unite with the masses, the more of the masses we unite with, the better.

"On the Chungking Negotiations" (October 17, 1945), Selected Works, Vol. IV, p. 59.

The army in the Liberated Areas must support the government and cherish the people, while the democratic governments must lead the people in the work of supporting the army and giving preferential treatment to the families of soldiers fighting Japan. In this way relations between the army and the people will become still better.

"On Coalition Government" (April 24, 1945), Selected Works, Vol. III, p. 311.

In the army the task of supporting the government and cherishing the people should be handled through the ideological education of every commander and fighter, so that they all thoroughly understand its importance. As long as the army on its part does this job well, the local government and the people will also improve their relations with the army.

"Policy for Work in the Liberated Areas for 1946" (December 15, 1945), Selected Works, Vol. IV, p. 77.

In the course of these campaigns, [1] the army on its side and the Party and the government on theirs should thoroughly examine the shortcomings and mistakes of 1943, and should resolutely correct them in 1944. From now on, such campaigns should be launched everywhere in the first month of every lunar year, and in the course of them the pledges to "support the government and cherish the people" and "support the army and give preferential treatment to the families of soldiers fighting Japan" should be read out time and again, and there should be repeated self-criticism before the masses of any high-handed behaviour by the troops in the base areas towards the Party or government personnel or towards civilians, or of any lack of concern for the troops shown by the Party or government personnel or the civilians (each side criticizing itself and not the other) in order that these shortcomings and mistakes may be thoroughly corrected.

"Spread the Campaigns to Reduce Rent, Increase Production and 'Support the Government and Cherish the People' in the Base Areas" (October 1, 1943), Selected Works, Vol. III, p. 135.

Note:

1. Campaigns to "support the government and cherish the people" and to "support the army and give preferential treatment to the families of soldiers fighting Japan".-- Tr.

15. DEMOCRACY IN THE THREE MAIN FIELDS

A proper measure of democracy should be put into effect in the army, chiefly by abolishing the feudal practice of bullying and beating and by having officers and men share weal and woe. Once this is done, unity will be achieved between officers and men, the combat effectiveness of the army will be greatly increased, and there will be no doubt of our ability to sustain the long, cruel war.

"On Protracted War" (May 1938), Selected Works, Vol. II, p. 186.

Apart from the role played by the Party, the reason why the Red Army has been able to carry on in spite of such poor material conditions and such frequent engagements is its practice of democracy. The officers do not beat the men; officers and men receive equal treatment; soldiers are free to hold meetings and to speak out; trivial formalities have been done away with; and the accounts are open for all to inspect.... In China the army needs democracy as much as the people do. Democracy in our army is an important weapon for undermining the feudal mercenary army.

"The Struggle in the Chingkang Mountains" (November 25, 1928), Selected Works, Vol. I, p. 83.

The policy for political work in our army units is fully to arouse the rank and file, the commanders and all working personnel in order to achieve three major objectives through a democratic movement under centralized leadership, namely, a high degree of political unity, better living conditions, and better military technique and tactics. The Three Check-ups and Three Improvements [1] now being enthusiastically carried out in our army units are intended to attain the first two of these objectives through the methods of political and economic democracy.

With regard to economic democracy, the representatives elected by the soldiers must be ensured the right to assist (but not to bypass) the company leadership in managing the company's supplies and mess.

With regard to military democracy, in periods of training there must be mutual instruction as between officers and soldiers and among the soldiers themselves; and in periods of fighting the companies at the front must hold big and small meetings of various kinds. Under the direction of the company leadership, the rank and file should be roused to discuss how to attack and capture enemy positions and how to fulfill other combat tasks. When the fighting lasts several days, several such meetings should be held. This kind of military democracy was practised with great success in the battle of Panlung in northern Shensi and in the battle of Shihchiachuang in the Shansi-Chahar-Hopei area. It has been proved that the practice can only do good and can do no harm whatsoever.

"The Democratic Movement in the Army" (January 30, 1948), Selected Military Writings, 2nd ed., p. 353.

In the present great struggle, the Chinese Communist Party demands that all its leading bodies and all its members and cadres should give the fullest expression to their initiative, which alone can ensure victory. This initiative must be demonstrated concretely in the ability of the leading bodies, the cadres and the Party rank and file to work creatively, in their readiness to assume responsibility, in the exuberant vigour they show in their work, in their courage and ability to raise questions, voice opinions and criticize defects, and in the comradely supervision that is maintained over the leading bodies and the leading cadres. Otherwise, "initiative" will be an empty thing. But the exercise of such initiative depends on the spread of democracy in Party life. It cannot be brought into play if there is not enough democracy in Party life. Only in an atmosphere of democracy can large numbers of able people be brought forward.

"The Role of the Chinese Communist Party in the National War" (October 1938), Selected Works, Vol. II, p. 204.

Anyone should be allowed to speak out, whoever he may be, so long as he is not a hostile element and does not make malicious attacks, and it does not matter if he says something wrong. Leaders at all levels have the duty to listen to others. Two principles must be observed: (1) Say all you know and say it without reserve; (2) Don't blame the speaker but take his words as a warning. Unless the principle of "Don't blame the speaker" is observed genuinely and not falsely, the result will not be "Say all you know and say it without reserve".

"The Tasks for 1945" (December 15, 1944).
Education in democracy must be carried on within the Party so that members can understand the meaning of democratic life, the meaning of the relationship between democracy and centralism, and the way in which democratic centralism should be put into practice. Only in this way can we really extend democracy within the Party and at the same time avoid ultra-democracy and the laissez-faire which destroys discipline.

"The Role of the Chinese Communist Party in the National War" (October 1938), Selected Works, Vol. II, p. 205.

Both in the army and in the local organizations, inner-Party democracy is meant to strengthen discipline and increase combat effectiveness, not to weaken them.

Ibid.

In the sphere of theory, destroy the roots of ultra-democracy. First, it should be pointed out that the danger of ultra-democracy lies in the fact that it damages or even completely wrecks the Party organization and weakens or even completely undermines the Party's fighting capacity, rendering the Party incapable of fulfilling its fighting tasks and thereby causing the defeat of the revolution. Next, it should be pointed out that the source of ultra-democracy consists in the petty bourgeoisie's individualistic aversion to discipline. When this characteristic is brought into the Party, it develops into ultra-democratic ideas politically and organizationally. These ideas are utterly incompatible with the fighting tasks of the proletariat.

"On Correcting Mistaken Ideas in the Party" (December 1929), Selected Works, Vol. I, p. 108.

Note:
1. The "Three Check-ups" and "Three Improvements" constituted an important movement for Party consolidation and for ideological education in the army which was carried out by our Party in conjunction with the land reform during the People's War of Liberation. In the localities, the "Three Check-ups" meant checking on class origin, ideology and style of work; in the armed units, the check-ups were on class origin, performance of duty and will to fight. The "Three Improvements" meant organizational consolidation, ideological education and rectification of style of work.

16. EDUCATION AND THE TRAINING OF TROOPS

Our educational policy must enable everyone who receives an education to develop morally, intellectually and physically and become a worker with both socialist consciousness and culture.

On the Correct Handling of Contradictions Among the People (February 27, 1959), 1st pocket ed., p. 44.

As for education for cadres whether at work or in schools for cadres, a policy should be established of focusing such education on the study of the practical problems of the Chinese revolution and using the basic principles of Marxism-Leninism as the guide, and the method of studying Marxism-Leninism statically and in isolation should be discarded.

"Reform Our Study" (May 1941), Selected Works, Vol. III, p. 24.

For a military school, the most important question is the selection of a director and instructors and the adoption of an educational policy.

"Problems of Strategy in China's Revolutionary War" (December 1936), Selected Works, Vol. I, p. 185.

A school of a hundred people certainly cannot be run well if it does not have a leading group of several people, or a dozen or more, which is formed in accordance with the actual circumstances (and not thrown together artificially) and is composed of the most active, upright and alert of the teachers, the other staff and the students.

"Some Questions Concerning Methods of Leadership" (June 1, 1943), Selected Works, Vol. III, pp. 118-19.

All officers and fighters of our army must improve their military art, march forward courageously towards certain victory in the war, and resolutely, thoroughly, wholly and completely wipe out all enemies.

"Manifesto of the Chinese People's Liberation Army" (October 1947), Selected Military Writings, 2nd ed., p. 340.

Equal importance should be attached to the military and political aspects of the one-year consolidation and training programme which has just begun, and the two aspects should be integrated. At the start, stress should be placed on the political aspect, on improving relations between officers and men, enhancing internal unity and arousing a high level of enthusiasm among the masses of cadres and fighters. Only thus will the military consolidation and training proceed smoothly and attain better results.

"The Tasks for 1945" (December 15, 1944).

As for the method of training, we should unfold the mass training movement in which officers teach soldiers, soldiers teach officers and the soldiers teach each other.

"Policy for Work in the Liberated Areas for 1946" (December 15, 1945), *Selected Works, Vol. IV, p. 76.*

Our slogan in training troops is, "Officers teach soldiers, soldiers teach officers and soldiers teach each other". The fighters have a lot of practical combat experience. The officers should learn from the fighters, and when they have made other people's experience their own, they will become more capable.

"A Talk to the Editorial Staff of the Shansi-Suiyuan Daily" (April 2, 1948), *Selected Works, Vol. IV, p. 243.*

As for the training courses, the main objective should still be to raise the level of technique in marksmanship, bayoneting grenade-throwing and the like and the secondary objective should be to raise the level of tactics, while special emphasis should be laid on night operations.

"Policy for Work in the Liberated Areas for 1946" (December 15, 1945), *Selected Works, Vol. IV, p. 76.*

17. SERVING THE PEOPLE

We should be modest and prudent, guard against arrogance and rashness, and serve the Chinese people heart and soul.

"China's Two Possible Destinies" (April 23, 1945), Selected Works, Vol. III p. 253.

Our point of departure is to serve the people whole-heartedly and never for a moment divorce ourselves from the masses, to proceed in all cases from the interests of the people and not from one's self-interest or from the interests of a small group, and to identify our responsibility to the people with our responsibility to the leading organs of the Party.

"On Coalition Government" (April 24, 1945), Selected Works, Vol. III, p. 315.

The organs of state must practise democratic centralism, they must rely on the masses and their personnel must serve the people.

On the Correct Handling of Contradictions Among the People (February 27, 1957), 1st pocket ed., p. 8.

Comrade Bethune's spirit, his utter devotion to others without any thought of self, was shown in his boundless sense of responsibility in his work and his boundless warm-heartedness towards all comrades and the people. Every Communist must learn from him.

We must all learn the spirit of absolute selflessness from him. With this spirit everyone can be very useful to the people. A man's ability may be great or small, but if he has this spirit, he is already noble-minded and pure, a man of moral integrity and above vulgar interests, a man who is of value to the people.

"In Memory of Norman Bethune" (December 21, 1939), Selected Works, Vol. II, pp. 337-38.

Our Communist Party and the Eighth Route and New Fourth Armies led by our Party are battalions of the revolution. These battalions of ours are wholly dedicated to the liberation of the people and work entirely in the people's interests.

"Serve the People" (September 8, 1944), Selected Works, Vol. III, p. 227.

All our cadres, whatever their rank, are servants of the people, and whatever we do is to serve the people. How then can we be reluctant to discard any of our bad traits?

"The Tasks for 1945" (December 15, 1944).

Our duty is to hold ourselves responsible to the people. Every word, every act and every policy must conform to the people's interests, and if mistakes occur, they must be corrected--that is what being responsible to the people means.

"The Situation and Our Policy After the Victory in the War of Resistance Against Japan" (August 13, 1945), Selected Works, Vol. IV, p. 16.

Wherever there is struggle there is sacrifice, and death is a common occurrence. But we have the interests of the people and the sufferings of the great majority at heart, and when we die for the people it is a worthy death. Nevertheless, we should do our best to avoid unnecessary sacrifices.

"Serve the People" (September 8, 1944), Selected Works, Vol. III, p. 228.

All men must die, but death can vary in its significance. The ancient Chinese writer Szuma Chien said, "Though death befalls all men alike, it may be weightier than Mount Tai or lighter than a feather." To die for the people is weightier than Mount Tai, but to work for the fascists and die for the exploiters and oppressors is lighter than a feather.

Ibid. p. 227.

18. PATRIOTISM AND INTERNATIONALISM

Can a Communist, who is an internationalist, at the same time be a patriot? We hold that he not only can be, but must be. The specific content of patriotism is determined by historical conditions. There is the "patriotism" of the Japanese aggressors and of Hitler, and there is our patriotism. Communists must resolutely oppose the "patriotism" of the Japanese aggressors and of Hitler. The Communists of Japan and Germany are defeatists with regard to the wars being waged by their countries. To bring about the defeat of the Japanese aggressors and of Hitler by every possible means is in the interests of the Japanese and the German people, and the more complete the defeat the better.... For the wars launched by the Japanese aggressors and Hitler are harming the people at home as well as the people of the world. China's case, however, is different, because she is the victim of aggression. Chinese Communists must therefore combine patriotism with internationalism. We are at once internationalists and patriots, and our slogan is, "Fight to defend the motherland against the aggressors." For us defeatism is a crime and to strive for victory in the War of Resistance is an inescapable duty. For only by fighting in defence of the motherland can we defeat the aggressors and achieve national liberation. And only by achieving national liberation will it be possible for the proletariat and other working people to achieve their own emancipation. The victory of China and the defeat of the invading imperialists will help the people of other countries. Thus, in wars of national liberation patriotism is applied internationalism.

"The Role of the Chinese Communist Party in the National War" (October 1938), Selected Works, Vol. II, p. 196.

What kind of spirit is this that makes a foreigner selflessly adopt the cause of the Chinese people's liberation as his own? It is the spirit of internationalism, the spirit of communism, from which every Chinese Communist must learn. We must unite with the proletariat of all the capitalist countries, with the proletariat of Japan, Britain, the United States, Germany, Italy and all other capitalist countries, before it is possible to overthrow imperialism, to liberate our nation and people, and to liberate the other nations and peoples of the world. This is our internationalism, the internationalism with which we oppose both narrow nationalism and narrow patriotism.
"In Memory of Norman Bethune" (December 21, 1939), Selected Works, Vol. II, p. 337.

In the fight for complete liberation the oppressed people rely first of all on their own struggle and then, and only then, on international assistance. The people who have triumphed in their own revolution should help those still struggling for liberation. This is our internationalist duty.

Talk with African friends (August 8, 1963).

The socialist countries are states of an entirely new type in which the exploiting classes have been overthrown and the working people are in power. The principle of integrating internationalism with patriotism is practised in the relations between these countries. We are closely bound by common interests and common ideals.

"Speech at the Meeting of the Supreme Soviet of the U.S.S.R. in Celebration of the 40th Anniversary of the Great October Socialist Revolution" (November 6, 1957).

The people of the countries in the socialist camp should unite, the people of the countries in Asia, Africa and Latin America should unite, the people of all the continents should unite, all peace-loving countries should unite, and all countries subjected to U.S. aggression, control, intervention or bullying should unite, and so form the broadest united front to oppose the U.S. imperialist policies of aggression and war and to defend world peace.

"Statement Supporting the Panamanian People's Just Patriotic Struggle Against U.S. Imperialism" (January 12, 1964), People of the World, Unite and Defeat the U.S. Aggressors and All Their Lackeys, 2nd ed., p. 9.

Things develop ceaselessly. It is only forty-five years since the Revolution of 19II, but the face of China has completely changed. In another forty-five years, that is, in the year 2001, or the beginning of the 21st century, China will have undergone an even greater change. She will have become a powerful socialist industrial country. And that is as it should be. China is a land with an area of 9,600,000 square kilometers and a population of 600 million people, and she ought to have made a greater contribution to humanity. Her contribution over a long period has been far too small. For this we are regretful.

But we must be modest--not only now, but forty-five years hence as well. We should always be modest. In our international relations, we Chinese people should get rid of great-power chauvinism resolutely, thoroughly, wholly and completely.

"In Commemoration of Dr. Sun Yat-sen" (November 1956).

We must never adopt an arrogant attitude of great-power chauvinism and become conceited because of the victory of our revolution and certain achievements in our construction. Every nation, big or small, has its strong and weak points.

"Opening Address at the Eighth National Congress of the Communist Party of China" (September 15, 1956).

19. REVOLUTIONARY HEROISM

This army has an indomitable spirit and is determined to vanquish all enemies and never to yield. No matter what the difficulties and hardships, so long as a single man remains, he will fight on.

"On Coalition Government" (April 24, 1945), Selected Works, Vol. III, p. 264.

Give full play to our style of fighting--courage in battle, no fear of sacrifice, no fear of fatigue, and continuous fighting (that is, fighting successive battles in a short time without rest).

"The Present Situation and Our Tasks" (December 25, 1947), Selected Works, Vol. IV, p. 161.

Thousands upon thousands of martyrs have heroically laid down their lives for the people; let us hold their banner high and march ahead along the path crimson with their blood!

"On Coalition Government" (April 24, 1945), Selected Works, Vol. III, p. 318.

Be resolute, fear no sacrifice and surmount every difficulty to win victory.

"The Foolish Old Man Who Removed the Mountains" (June 11, 1945), Selected Works, Vol. III, p. 321.

At a critical moment in the progress of the Northern Expedition, . . . the treacherous and reactionary policies of "party purge" and massacre adopted by the Kuomintang authorities wrecked this national united front--the united front of the Kuomintang, the Communist Party and all sections of the people, which embodied the Chinese people's cause of liberation--and all its revolutionary policies. Thereupon, unity was replaced by civil war, democracy by dictatorship, and a China full of brightness by a China covered in darkness. But the Chinese Communist Party and the Chinese people were neither cowed nor conquered nor exterminated. They picked themselves up, wiped off the blood, buried their fallen comrades and went into battle again. Holding high the great standard of revolution, they rose in armed resistance and over a vast territory in China they set up people's governments, carried out land reform, built up a people's army--the Chinese Red Army--and preserved and expanded the revolutionary forces of the Chinese people.

"On Coalition Government" (April 24, 1945), Selected Works, Vol. III, p. 261.

You have many good qualities and have rendered great service, but you must always remember not to become conceited. You are respected by all, and quite rightly, but this easily leads to conceit. If you become conceited, if you are not modest and cease to exert yourselves, and if you do not respect others, do not respect the cadres and the masses, then you will cease to be heroes and models. There have been such people in the past, and I hope you will not follow their example.

"We Must Learn to Do Economic Work" (January 10, 1945), Selected Works, Vol. III, p. 239.

In the fight to wipe out the enemy and to restore and increase industrial and agricultural production, you have overcome many difficulties and hardships and demonstrated immense courage, wisdom and initiative. You are models for the whole Chinese nation, the backbone of the victorious advance of the people's cause in all spheres, pillars of support to the People's Government and bridges linking the People's Government with the great masses.

Message of greetings on behalf of the Central Committee of the Chinese Communist Party to the Meeting of Representatives of National Combat Heroes and Model Workers (September 25, 1950).

We the Chinese nation have the spirit to fight the enemy to the last drop of our blood, the determination to recover our lost territory by our own efforts, and the ability to stand on our own feet in the family of nations.

"On Tactics Against Japanese Imperialism" (December 27, 1935), Selected Works, Vol. I, p. 170.

20. BUILDING OUR COUNTRY THROUGH DILIGENCE AND FRUGALITY

We must see to it that all our cadres and all our people constantly bear in mind that ours is a big socialist country but an economically backward and poor one, and that this is a very great contradiction. To make China rich and strong needs several decades of intense effort, which will include, among other things, the effort to practise strict economy and combat waste, i.e., the policy of building up our country through diligence and frugality.

On the Correct Handling of Contradictions Among the People (February 27, 1957), 1st pocket ed., p. 71.

Diligence and frugality should be practised in running factories and shops and all state-owned, co-operative and other enterprises. The principle of diligence and frugality should be observed in everything. This principle of economy is one of the basic principles of socialist economics. China is a big country, but she is still very poor. It will take several decades to make China prosperous. Even then we will still have to observe the principle of diligence and frugality. But it is in the coming few decades, during the present series of five-year plans, that we must particularly advocate diligence and frugality, that we must pay special attention to economy.

Introductory note to "Running a Co-operative Diligently and Frugally" (1955), The Socialist Upsurge in China's Countryside, Chinese ed., Vol. I.

Wherever we happen to be, we must treasure our manpower and material resources, and must not take a short view and indulge in wastefulness and extravagance. Wherever we are, from the very first year of our work we must bear in mind the many years to come, the protracted war that must be maintained, the counter-offensive, and the work of reconstruction after the enemy's expulsion. On the one hand, never be wasteful or extravagant; on the other, actively expand production. Previously, in some places people suffered a great deal because they did not take the long view and neglected economy in manpower and material resources and the expansion of production. The lesson is there and attention must be called to it.

"We Must Learn to Do Economic Work" (January 10, 1945), Selected Works, Vol. III, p. 244.

In order to speed up this restoration and development of agricultural production and industrial production in small towns], we must do our utmost, in the course of our struggle for the abolition of the feudal system, to preserve all useful means of production and of livelihood, take resolute measures against anyone's destroying or wasting them, oppose extravagant eating and drinking and pay attention to thrift and economy.

"Speech at a Conference of Cadres in the Shansi-Suiyuan Liberated Area" (April 1, 1948), Selected Works, Vol. IV, p. 238.

Thrift should be the guiding principle in our government expenditure. It should be made clear to all government workers that corruption and waste are very great crimes. Our campaigns against corruption and waste have already achieved some results, but further efforts are required. Our system of accounting must be guided by the principle of saving every copper for the war effort, for the revolutionary cause and for our economic construction.

"Our Economic Policy" (January 23, 1934), Selected Works, Vol. I, p. 145.

A dangerous tendency has shown itself of late among many of our personnel--an unwillingness to share the joys and hardships of the masses, a concern for personal fame and gain. This is very bad. One way of overcoming it is to simplify our organizations in the course of our campaign to increase production and practise economy, and to transfer cadres to lower levels so that a considerable number will return to productive work.

On the Correct Handling of Contradictions Among the People (February 27, 1957), 1st pocket ed., p 71.

Production by the army for its own support has not only improved the army's living conditions and lightened the burden on the people, thereby making it possible further to expand the army. In addition, it has had many immediate side effects. They are as follows:
(1) Improved relations between officers and men. Officers and men work together in production and become like brothers.
(2) Better attitude to labour. Since the army began to produce for its own support, the attitude to labour has improved and loafer ways have been overcome.
(3) Strengthened discipline. Far from weakening discipline in battle and in army life, labour discipline in production actually strengthens it.
(4) Improved relations between the army and the people. Once an armed force begins to "keep house" for itself, encroachments upon the property of the people seldom or never occur. As the army and the people exchange labour and help each other in production, the friendship between them is strengthened.
(5) Less grumbling in the army about the government and improved relations between the two.
(6) An impetus to the great production campaign of the people. Once the army engages in production, the need for government and other organizations to do likewise becomes more obvious, and they do so more energetically; also, the need for a universal campaign of the whole people to increase production naturally becomes more obvious, and this too is carried on more energetically.

"On Production by the Army for Its Own Support and on the Importance of the Great Movements for Rectification and for Production" (April 27, 1945), Selected Works, Vol. III, pp. 327-28.

Some people say that if the army units go in for production, they will be unable to train or fight and that if the government and other organizations do so, they will be unable to do their own work. This is a false argument. In recent years our army units in the Border Region have undertaken production on a big scale to provide themselves with ample food and clothing and have simultaneously done their training and conducted their political studies and literacy and other courses much more successfully than before, and there is greater unity than ever within the army and between the army and the people. While there was a large-scale production campaign at the front last year, great successes were gained in the fighting and in addition an extensive training campaign was started. And thanks to production, the personnel of the government and other organizations live a better life and work with greater devotion and efficiency; this is the case both in the Border Region and at the front.

"We Must Learn to Do Economic Work" (January 10, 1945), Selected Works, Vol. III, pp. 243-44.

21. SELF-RELIANCE AND ARDUOUS STRUGGLE

On what basis should our policy rest? It should rest on our own strength, and that means regeneration through one's own efforts. We are not alone; all the countries and people in the world opposed to imperialism are our friends. Nevertheless, we stress regeneration through our own efforts. Relying on the forces we ourselves organize, we can defeat all Chinese and foreign reactionaries.

"The Situation and Our Policy After the Victory in the War of Resistance Against Japan" (August 13, 1945), Selected Works, Vol. IV, p. 20.

We stand for self-reliance. We hope for foreign aid but cannot be dependent on it; we depend on our own efforts, on the creative power of the whole army and the entire people.

"We Must Learn to Do Economic Work" (January 10, 1945), Selected Works, Vol. III, p. 241.

To win countrywide victory is only the first step in a long march of ten thousand miles. The Chinese revolution is great, but the road after the revolution will be longer, the work greater and more arduous. This must be made clear now in the Party. The comrades must be helped to remain modest, prudent and free from arrogance and rashness in their style of work. The comrades must be helped to preserve the style of plain living and hard struggle.

"Report to the Second Plenary Session of the Seventh Central Committee of the Communist Party of China (March 5, 1949), Selected Works, Vol. IV, p. 374.

We must thoroughly clear away all ideas among our cadres of winning easy victories through good luck, without hard and bitter struggle, without sweat and blood.

"Build Stable Base Areas in the Northeast" (December 28, 1945), Selected Works, Vol. IV, p. 84.

We should carry on constant propaganda among the people on the facts of world progress and the bright future ahead so that they will build their confidence in victory. At the same time, we must tell the people and tell our comrades that there will be twists and turns in our road, There are still many obstacles and difficulties along the road of revolution. The Seventh Congress of our Party assumed that the difficulties would be many, for we preferred to assume there would be more difficulties rather than less. Some comrades do not like to think much about difficulties. But difficulties are facts; we must recognize as many difficulties as there are and should not adopt a "policy of non-recognition". We must recognize difficulties, analyse them and combat them. There are no straight roads in the world; we must be prepared to follow a road which twists and turns and not try to get things on the cheap. It must not be imagined that one fine morning all the reactionaries will go down on their knees of their own accord. In a word, while the prospects are bright, the road has twists and turns. There are still many difficulties ahead which we must not overlook. By uniting with the entire people in a common effort, we can certainly overcome all difficulties and win victory.

"On the Chungking Negotiations" (October 17, 1945), Selected Works, Vol. IV, pp. 59-60.

Anyone who sees only the bright side but not the difficulties cannot fight effectively for the accomplishment of the Party's tasks.

"On Coalition Government" (April 24, 1945), Selected Works, Vol. III, p. 314.

The wealth of society is created by the workers, peasants and working intellectuals. If they take their destiny into their own hands, follow a Marxist-Leninist line and take an active attitude in solving problems instead of evading them, there will be no difficulty in the world which they cannot overcome.

Introductory note to "The Party Secretary Takes the Lead and All the Party Members Help Run the Co-operatives" (1955), The Socialist Upsurge in China's Countryside, Chinese ed., Vol. I.

The comrades throughout the Party must take all this fully into account and be prepared to overcome all difficulties with an indomitable will and in a planned way. The reactionary forces and we both have difficulties. But the difficulties of the reactionary forces are insurmountable because they are forces on the verge of death and have no future. Our difficulties can be overcome because we are new and rising forces and have a bright future.

"Greet the New High Tide of the Chinese Revolution" (February 1, 1947), Selected Works, Vol. IV, p. 125.

In times of difficulty we must not lose sight of our achievements, must see the bright future and must pluck up our courage.

"Serve the People" (September 8, 1944), Selected Works, Vol. III, pp. 227-28.

New things always have to experience difficulties and setbacks as they grow. It is sheer fantasy to imagine that the cause of socialism is all plain sailing and easy success, without difficulties and setbacks or the exertion of tremendous efforts.

On the Correct Handling of Contradictions Among the People (February 27, 1957), 1st pocket ed., pp. 32-33.

At certain times in the revolutionary struggle, the difficulties outweigh the favourable conditions and so constitute the principal aspect of the contradiction and the favourable conditions constitute the secondary aspect. But through their efforts the revolutionaries can overcome the difficulties step-by-step and open up a favourable new situation, thus a difficult situation yields place to a favourable one.

"On Contradiction" (August 1937), Selected Works, Vol. I, p. 335.

What is work? Work is struggle. There are difficulties and problems in those places for us to overcome and solve. We go there to work and struggle to overcome these difficulties. A good comrade is one who is more eager to go where the difficulties are greater.

"On the Chungking Negotiations" (October 17, 1945), Selected Works, Vol. IV, p. 58.

There is an ancient Chinese fable called "The Foolish Old Man Who Removed the Mountains". It tells of an old man who lived in northern China long, long ago and was known as the Foolish Old Man of North Mountain. His house faced south and beyond his doorway stood the two great peaks, Taihang and Wangwu, obstructing the way. With great determination, he led his sons in digging up these mountains hoe in hand. Another greybeard, known as the Wise Old Man, saw them and said derisively, "How silly of you to do this! It is quite impossible for you few to dig up these two huge mountains." The Foolish Old Man replied, "When I die, my sons will carry on; when they die, there will be my grandsons, and then their sons and grandsons, and so on to infinity. High as they are, the mountains cannot grow any higher and with every bit we dig, they will be that much lower. Why can't we clear them away?" Having refuted the Wise Old Man's wrong view, he went on digging every day, unshaken in his conviction. God was moved by this and he sent down two angels, who carried the mountains away on their backs. Today, two big mountains lie like a dead weight on the Chinese people. One is imperialism; the other is feudalism. The Chinese Communist Party has long made up its mind to dig them up. We must persevere and work unceasingly, and we, too, will touch God's heart. Our God is none other than the masses of the Chinese people. If they stand up and dig together with us, why can't these two mountains be cleared away?

"The Foolish Old Man Who Removed the Mountains" (June 11, 1945), Selected Works, Vol. III, p. 322.

22. METHODS OF THINKING AND METHODS OF WORK

The history of mankind is one of continuous development from the realm of necessity to the realm of freedom. This process is never-ending. In any society in which classes exist class struggle will never end. In classless society the struggle between the new and the old and between truth and falsehood will never end. In the fields of the struggle for production and scientific experiment, mankind makes constant progress and nature undergoes constant change, they never remain at the same level. Therefore, man has constantly to sum up experience and go on discovering, inventing, creating and advancing. Ideas of stagnation, pessimism, inertia and complacency are all wrong. They are wrong because they agree neither with the historical facts of social development over the past million years, nor with the historical facts of nature so far known to us (i.e., nature as revealed in the history of celestial bodies, the earth, life, and other natural phenomena).

Quoted in "Premier Chou Enlai's Report on the Work of the Government to the First Session of the Third National People's Congress of the People's Republic of China" (December 21-22, 1964).

Natural science is one of man's weapons in his fight for freedom. For the purpose of attaining freedom in society, man must use social science to understand and change society and carry out social revolution. For the purpose of attaining freedom in the world of nature, man must use natural science to understand, conquer and change nature and thus attain freedom from nature.

Speech at the inaugural meeting of the Natural Science Research Society of the Border Region (February 5, 1940).

The Marxist philosophy of dialectical materialism has two outstanding characteristics. One is its class nature: it openly avows that dialectical materialism is in the service of the proletariat. The other is its practicality: it emphasizes the dependence of theory on practice, emphasizes that theory is based on practice and in turn serves practice.

"On Practice" (July 1937), Selected Works, Vol. I, p. 297.
Marxist philosophy holds that the most important problem does not lie in understanding the laws of the objective world and thus being able to explain it, but in applying the knowledge of these laws actively to change the world.

Ibid. p. 304.

Where do correct ideas come from? Do they drop from the skies? No. Are they innate in the mind? No. They come from social practice, and from it alone; they come from three kinds of social practice, the struggle for production, the class struggle and scientific experiment.

Where Do Correct Ideas Come from? (May 1963), 1st pocket ed., p. 1.

It is man's social being that determines his thinking. Once the correct ideas characteristic of the advanced class are grasped by the masses, these ideas turn into a material force which changes society and changes the world.

Ibid.

In their social practice, men engage in various kinds of struggle and gain rich experience, both from their successes and from their failures. Countless phenomena of the objective external world are reflected in a man's brain through his five sense organs--the organs of sight, hearing, smell, taste and touch. At first, knowledge is perceptual. The leap to conceptual knowledge, i.e., to ideas, occurs when sufficient perceptual knowledge is accumulated. This is one process in cognition. It is the first stage in the whole process of cognition, the stage leading from objective matter to subjective consciousness, from existence to ideas. Whether or not one's consciousness or ideas (including theories, policies, plans or measures) do correctly reflect the laws of the objective external world is not yet proved at this stage, in which it is not yet possible to ascertain whether they are correct or not. Then comes the second stage in the process of cognition, the stage leading from consciousness back to matter, from ideas back to existence, in which the knowledge gained in the first stage is applied in social practice to ascertain whether the theories, policies, plans or measures meet with the anticipated success. Generally speaking, those that succeed are correct and those that fail are incorrect, and this is especially true of man's struggle with nature. In social struggle, the forces representing the advanced class sometimes suffer defeat not because their ideas are incorrect but because, in the balance of forces engaged in struggle, they are not as powerful for the time being as the forces of reaction; they are therefore temporarily defeated, but they are bound to triumph sooner or later. Man's knowledge makes another leap through the test of practice. This leap is more important than the previous one. For it is this leap alone that can prove the correctness or incorrectness of the first leap in cognition, i.e., of the ideas, theories, policies, plans or measures formulated in the course of reflecting the objective external world. There is no other way of testing truth.

Ibid. pp. 1-3.

Often, correct knowledge can be arrived at only after many repetitions of the process leading from matter to consciousness and then back to matter, that is, leading from practice to knowledge and then back to practice. Such is the Marxist theory of knowledge, the dialectical materialist theory of knowledge.

Ibid. p. 3.

Whoever wants to know a thing has no way of doing so except by coming into contact with it, that is, by living (practising) in its environment. If you want knowledge, you must take part in the practice of changing reality. If you want to know the taste of a pear, you must change the pear by eating it yourself. If you want to know the theory and methods of revolution, you must take part in revolution. All genuine knowledge originates in direct experience.

"On Practice" (July 1937), Selected Works, Vol. I, pp. 299-300.

Knowledge begins with practice, and theoretical knowledge which is acquired through practice must then return to practice. The active function of knowledge manifests itself not only in the active leap from perceptual to rational knowledge, but--and this is more important--it must manifest itself in the leap from rational knowledge to revolutionary practice.

Ibid. p. 304.

It is well known that when you do anything, unless you understand its actual circumstances, its nature and its relations to other things, you will not know the laws governing it, or know how to do it, or be able to do it well.

"Problems of Strategy in China's Revolutionary War" (December 1936), Selected Works, Vol. I, p. 179.

If a man wants to succeed in his work, that is, to achieve the anticipated results, he must bring his ideas into correspondence with the laws of the objective external world; if they do not correspond, he will fail in his practice. After he fails, he draws his lessons, corrects his ideas to make them correspond to the laws of the external world, and can thus turn failure into success; this is what is meant by "failure is the mother of success" and "a fall into the pit, a gain in your wit".

"On Practice" (July 1937), Selected Works, Vol. I, pp. 296-97.

We are Marxists, and Marxism teaches that in our approach to a problem we should start from objective facts, not from abstract definitions, and that we should derive our guiding principles, policies and measures from an analysis of these facts.

"Talks at the Yenan Forum on Literature and Art" (May 1942), Selected Works, Vol. III, p. 74.

The most fundamental method of work which all Communists must firmly bear in mind is to determine our working policies according to actual conditions. When we study the causes of the mistakes we have made, we find that they all arose because we departed from the actual situation at a given time and place and were subjective in determining our working policies.

"Speech at a Conference of Cadres in the Shansi-Suiyuan Liberated Area" (April 1, 1948), Selected Works, Vol. IV, pp. 229-30.

Idealism and metaphysics are the easiest things in the world, because people can talk as much nonsense as they like without basing it on objective reality or having it tested against reality. Materialism and dialectics, on the other hand, need effort. They must be based on and tested by objective reality. Unless one makes the effort one is liable to slip into idealism and metaphysics.

Introductory note to "Material on the Hu Feng Counter-Revolutionary Clique" (May 1955).

When we look at a thing, we must examine its essence and treat its appearance merely as an usher at the threshold, and once we cross the threshold, we must grasp the essence of the thing; this is the only reliable and scientific method of analysis.

"A Single Spark Can Start a Prairie Fire" (January 5, 1930), Selected Works, Vol. I, p. 119.

The fundamental cause of the development of a thing is not external but internal; it lies in the contradictoriness within the thing. This internal contradiction exists in every single thing, hence its motion and development. Contradictoriness within a thing is the fundamental cause of its development, while its interrelations and interactions with other things are secondary causes.

"On Contradiction" (August 1937), Selected Works, Vol. I, p. 313.

It [materialist dialectics] holds that external causes are the condition of change and internal causes are the basis of change, and that external causes become operative through internal causes. In a suitable temperature an egg changes into a chicken, but no temperature can change a stone into a chicken, because each has a different basis.

Ibid. p. 314.

Marxist philosophy holds that the law of the unity of opposites is the fundamental law of the universe. This law operates universally, whether in the natural world, in human society, or in man's thinking. Between the opposites in a contradiction there is at once unity and struggle, and it is this that impels things to move and change. Contradictions exist everywhere, but they differ in accordance with the different nature of different things. In any given phenomenon or thing, the unity of opposites is conditional, temporary and transitory, and hence relative, whereas the struggle of opposites is absolute.

On the Correct Handling of Contradictions Among the People (February 27, 1957), 1st pocket ed., p. 18.

The analytical method is dialectical. By analysis, we mean analysing the contradictions in things. And sound analysis is impossible without intimate knowledge of life and without real understanding of the pertinent contradictions.

Speech at the Chinese Communist Party's National Conference on Propaganda Work (March 12, 1957), 15t pocket ed., p. 20.

Concrete analysis of concrete conditions, Lenin said, is "the most essential thing in Marxism, the living soul of Marxism". Lacking an analytical approach, many of our comrades do not want to go deeply into complex matters, to analyse and study them over and over again, but like to draw simple conclusions which are either absolutely affirmative or absolutely negative. From now on we should remedy this state of affairs.

"Our Study and the Current Situation" (April 12, 1944), Selected Works, Vol. III, p. 165.

The way these comrades look at problems is wrong. They do not look at the essential or main aspects but emphasize the non-essential or minor ones. It should be pointed out that these non-essential or minor aspects must not be overlooked and must be dealt with one by one. But they should not be taken as the essential or main aspects, or we will lose our bearings.

On the Question of Agricultural Co-operation (July 31, 1955), 3rd ed., pp. 17-18.

In this world, things are complicated and are decided by many factors. We should look at problems from different aspects, not from just one.

"On the Chungking Negotiations" (October 17, 1945), Selected Works, Vol. IV, p. 54.

Only those who are subjective, one-sided and superficial in their approach to problems will smugly issue orders or directives the moment they arrive on the scene, without considering the circumstances, without viewing things in their totality (their history and their present state as a whole) and without getting to the essence of things (their nature and the internal relations between one thing and another). Such people are bound to trip and fall.

"On Practice" (July 1937), Selected Works, Vol. I, p. 302.

In studying a problem, we must shun subjectivity, one-sidedness and superficiality. To be subjective means not to look at problems objectively, that is, not to use the materialist viewpoint in looking at problems. I have discussed this in my essay "On Practice". To be one-sided means not to look at problems all-sidedly. Or it may be called seeing the part but not the whole, seeing the trees but not the forest. That way it is impossible to find the method for resolving a contradiction, it is impossible to accomplish the tasks of the revolution, to carry out assignments well or to develop inner-Party ideological struggle correctly. When Sun Wu Tzu said in discussing military science, "Know the enemy and know yourself, and you can fight a hundred battles with no danger of defeat", he was referring to the two sides in a battle. Wei Cheng of the Tang Dynasty also understood the error of one-sidedness when he said, "Listen to both sides and you will be enlightened, heed only one side and you will be benighted." But our comrades often look at problems one-sidedly, and so they often run into snags. Lenin said: "...in order really to know an object we must embrace, study, all its sides, all connections and "mediations". We shall never achieve this completely, but the demand for all-sidedness is a safeguard against mistakes and rigidity.

We should remember his words. To be superficial means to consider neither the characteristics of a contradiction in its totality nor the characteristics of each of its aspects; it means to deny the necessity for probing deeply into a thing and minutely studying the characteristics of its contradiction, but instead merely to look from afar and, after glimpsing the rough outline, immediately to try to resolve the contradiction (to answer a question, settle a dispute, handle work, or direct a military operation). This way of doing things is bound to lead to trouble. To be one-sided and superficial is at the same time to be subjective. For all objective things are actually interconnected and are governed by inner laws, but, instead of undertaking the task of reflecting things as they really are, some people only look at things one-sidedly or superficially and know neither their interconnections nor their inner laws, and so their method is subjectivist.

"On Contradiction" (August 1937), Selected Works, Vol. I, pp. 323-24.

One-sidedness means thinking in terms of absolutes, that is, a metaphysical approach to problems. In the appraisal of our work, it is one-sided to regard everything either as all positive or as all negative. To regard everything as positive is to see only the good and not the bad, and to tolerate only praise and no criticism. To talk as though our work is good in every respect is at variance with the facts. It is not true that everything is good; there are still shortcomings and mistakes. But neither is it true that everything is bad, and that, too, is at variance with the facts. Here analysis is necessary. To negate everything is to think, without having made any analysis, that nothing has been done well and that the great work of socialist construction, the great struggle in which hundreds of millions of people are participating, is a complete mess with nothing in it worth commending. Although there is a difference between the many people who hold such views and those who are hostile to the socialist system, these views are very mistaken and harmful and can only dishearten people. It is wrong to appraise our work either from the viewpoint that everything is positive, or from the viewpoint that everything is negative.

Speech at the Chinese Communist Party's National Conference on Propaganda Work (March 12, 1957), 1st pocket ed., pp. 16-17.

In approaching a problem a Marxist should see the whole as well as the parts. A frog in a well says, "The sky is no bigger than the mouth of the well." That is untrue, for the sky is not just the size of the mouth of the well. If it said, "A part of the sky is the size of the mouth of a well", that would be true, for it tallies with the facts.

"On Tactics Against Japanese Imperialism" (December 27, 1935), Selected Works, Vol. I, p. 159.

We must learn to look at problems all-sidedly, seeing the reverse as well as the obverse side of things. In given conditions, a bad thing can lead to good results and a good thing to bad results.
On the Correct Handling of Contradictions Among the People (February 27, 1957), 1st pocket ed., pp. 66-67.

While we recognize that in the general development of history the material determines the mental and social being determines social consciousness, we also--and indeed must--recognize the reaction of mental on material things, of social consciousness on social being and of the superstructure on the economic base. This does not go against materialism; on the contrary, it avoids mechanical materialism and firmly upholds dialectical materialism.

"On Contradiction" (August 1937), Selected Works, Vol. I, p. 336.

In seeking victory, those who direct a war cannot overstep the limitations imposed by the objective conditions; within these limitations, however, they can and must play a dynamic role in striving for victory. The stage of action for commanders in a war must be built upon objective possibilities, but on that stage they can direct the performance of many a drama, full of sound and colour, power and grandeur.

"On Protracted War" (May 1938), Selected Works, Vol. II, p. 152.

People must adapt their thinking to the changed conditions. Of course no one should go off into wild flights of fancy, or make plans of action unwarranted by the objective situation, or stretch for the impossible. The problem today, however, is that Rightist conservative thinking is still causing mischief in many spheres and preventing the work in these spheres from keeping pace with the development of the objective situation. The present problem is that many people consider it impossible to accomplish things which could be accomplished if they exerted themselves.

Preface to The Socialist Upsurge in China's Countryside (December 27, 1955), Chinese ed., Vol. I.

We should always use our brains and think everything over carefully. A common saying goes, "Knit your brows and you will hit upon a stratagem." In other words much thinking yields wisdom.

In order to get rid of the blindness which exists to a serious extent in our Party, we must encourage our comrades to think, to learn the method of analysis and to cultivate the habit of analysis.

"Our Study and the Current Situation" (April 12, 1944), Selected Works, Vol. III, pp. 174-75.

If in any process there are a number of contradictions, one of them must be the principal contradiction playing the leading and decisive role, while the rest occupy a secondary and subordinate position. Therefore, in studying any complex process in which there are two or more contradictions, we must devote every effort to finding its principal contradiction. Once this principal contradiction is grasped, all problems can be readily solved.

"On Contradiction" (August 1937), Selected Works, Vol. I, p. 332.

Of the two contradictory aspects, one must be principal and the other secondary. The principal aspect is the one playing the leading role in the contradiction. The nature of a thing is determined mainly by the principal aspect of a contradiction, the aspect which has gained the dominant position.

But this situation is not static; the principal and the non-principal aspects of a contradiction transform themselves into each other and the nature of the thing changes accordingly.

Ibid. p. 333.

It is not enough to set tasks, we must also solve the problem of the methods for carrying them out. If our task is to cross a river, we cannot cross it without a bridge or a boat. Unless the bridge or boat problem is solved, it is idle to speak of crossing the river. Unless the problem of method is solved, talk about the task is useless.

"Be Concerned with the Well-Being of the Masses, Pay Attention to Methods of Work" (January 27, 1934), Selected Works, Vol. I, p. 150.

In any task, if no general and widespread call is issued, the broad masses cannot be mobilized for action. But if persons in leading positions confine themselves to a general call--if they do not personally, in some of the organizations, go deeply and concretely into the work called for, make a break-through at some single point, gain experience and use this experience for guiding other units--then they will have no way of testing the correctness or of enriching the content of their general call, and there is the danger that nothing may come of it.

"Some Questions Concerning Methods of Leadership" (June 1, 1943), Selected Works, Vol. III, p. 117.

No one in a leading position is competent to give general guidance to all the units unless he derives concrete experience from particular individuals and events in particular subordinate units. This method must be promoted everywhere so that leading cadres at all levels learn to apply it.

Ibid. p. 118.

In any given place, there cannot be a number of central tasks at the same time. At any one time there can be only one central task, supplemented by other tasks of a second or third order of importance. Consequently, the person with over-all responsibility in the locality must take into account the history and circumstances of the struggle there and put the different tasks in their proper order; he should not act upon each instruction as it comes from the higher organization without any planning of his own, and thereby create a multitude of "central tasks" and a state of confusion and disorder. Nor should a higher organization simultaneously assign many tasks to a lower organization without indicating their relative importance and urgency or without specifying which is central, for that will lead to confusion in the steps to be taken by the lower organizations in their work and thus no definite results will be achieved. It is part of the art of leadership to take the whole situation into account and plan accordingly in the light of the historical conditions and existing circumstances of each locality, decide correctly on the centre of gravity and the sequence of the work for each period, steadfastly carry through the decision, and make sure that definite results are achieved.

Ibid. p. 121.

It [a regional or sub-regional bureau of the Central Committee of the Party] should constantly have a grip on the progress of the work, exchange experience and correct mistakes; it should not wait several months, half a year or a year before holding summing-up meetings for a general check-up and a general correction of mistakes. Waiting leads to great loss, while correcting mistakes as soon as they occur reduces loss.

"On the Policy Concerning Industry and Commerce" (February 27, 1948), Selected Works, Vol. IV, p. 204.

Don't wait until problems pile up and cause a lot of trouble before trying to solve them. Leaders must march ahead of the movement, not lag behind it.

Introductory note to "Contract on a Seasonal Basis" (1955), The Socialist Upsurge in China's Countryside, Chinese ed., Vol. III.

What we need is an enthusiastic but calm state of mind and intense but orderly work.

"Problems of Strategy in China's Revolutionary War" (December 1936), Selected Works, Vol. I, p. 211.

23. INVESTIGATION AND STUDY

Everyone engaged in practical work must investigate conditions at the lower levels. Such investigation is especially necessary for those who know theory but do not know the actual conditions, for otherwise they will not be able to link theory with practice. Although my assertion, "No investigation, no right to speak", has been ridiculed as "narrow empiricism", to this day I do not regret having made it; far from regretting it, I still insist that without investigation there cannot possibly be any right to speak. There are many people who "the moment they alight from the official carriage" make a hullabaloo, spout opinions, criticize this and condemn that; but, in fact, ten out of ten of them will meet with failure. For such views or criticisms, which are not based on thorough investigation, are nothing but ignorant twaddle. Countless times our Party suffered at the hands of these "imperial envoys" who rushed here, there and everywhere. Stalin rightly says that, "theory becomes purposeless if it is not connected with revolutionary practice". And he rightly adds that, "practice gropes in the dark if its path is not illumined by revolutionary theory". Nobody should be labeled a "narrow empiricist" except the "practical man" who gropes in the dark and lacks perspective and foresight.

"Preface and Postscript to Rural Surveys" (March and April 1941), Selected Works, Vol. III, p. 13.

To take such an attitude is to seek truth from facts. "Facts" are all the things that exist objectively, "truth" means their internal relations--that is, the laws governing them--and "to seek" means to study. We should proceed from the actual conditions inside and outside the country, the province, county or district, and derive from them, as our guide to action, laws which are inherent in them and not imaginary, that is, we should find the internal relations of the events occurring around us. And in order to do that we must rely not on subjective imagination, not on momentary enthusiasm, not on lifeless books, but on facts that exist objectively; we must appropriate the material in detail and, guided by the general principles of Marxism-Leninism, draw correct conclusions from it.

"Reform Our Study" (May 1941), Selected Works, Vol. III, pp. 22-23.
To behave like "a blindfolded man catching sparrows", or "a blind man groping for fish", to be crude and careless, to indulge in verbiage, to rest content with a smattering of knowledge--such is the extremely bad style of work that still exists among many comrades in our Party, a style utterly opposed to the fundamental spirit of Marxism-Leninism. Marx, Engels, Lenin and Stalin have taught us that it is necessary to study conditions conscientiously and to proceed from objective reality and not from subjective wishes; but many of our comrades act in direct violation of this truth.

Ibid. p. 18.

You can't solve a problem? Well, get down and investigate the present facts and its past history! When you have investigated the problem thoroughly, you will know how to solve it. Conclusions invariably come after investigation, and not before. Only a blockhead cudgels his brains on his own, or together with a group, to "find a solution" or "evolve an idea" without making any investigation. It must be stressed that this cannot possibly lead to any effective solution or any good idea.

Oppose Book Worship (May 1930), 1st pocket ed., p. 2.

Investigation may be likened to the long months of pregnancy, and solving a problem to the day of birth. To investigate a problem is, indeed, to solve it.

Ibid. p. 3.

[With the Marxist-Leninist attitude,] a person applies the theory and method of Marxism-Leninism to the systematic and thorough investigation and study of the environment. He does not work by enthusiasm alone but, as Stalin says, combines revolutionary sweep with practicalness.

"Reform Our Study" (May 1941), Selected Works, Vol. III, p. 22.

The only way to know conditions is to make social investigations, to investigate the conditions of each social class in real life. For those charged with directing work, the basic method for knowing conditions is to concentrate on a few cities and villages according to a plan and, using the fundamental viewpoint of Marxism, i.e., the method of class analysis, make a number of thorough investigations.

"Preface and Postscript to Rural Surveys" (March and April 1941), Selected Works, Vol. III, p. 11.

A fact-finding meeting need not be large; from three to five or seven or eight people are enough. Ample time must be allowed and an outline for the investigation must be prepared; furthermore, one must personally ask questions, take notes and have discussions with those at the meeting. Therefore one certainly cannot make an investigation, or do it well, without zeal, a determination to direct one's eyes downward and a thirst for knowledge, and without shedding the ugly mantle of pretentiousness and becoming a willing pupil.

Ibid. p. 12.

A commander's correct dispositions stem from his correct decisions, his correct decisions stem from his correct judgments, and his correct judgments stem from a thorough and necessary reconnaissance and from pondering on and piecing together the data of various kinds gathered through reconnaissance. He applies all possible and necessary methods of reconnaissance, and ponders on the information gathered about the enemy's situation, discarding the dross and selecting the essential, eliminating the false and retaining the true, proceeding from the one to the other and from the outside to the inside; then, he takes the conditions on his own side into account, and makes a study of both sides and their interrelations, thereby forming his judgments, making up his mind and working out his plans. Such is the complete process of knowing a situation which a military man goes through before he formulates a strategic plan, a campaign plan or a battle plan.

"Problems of Strategy in China's Revolutionary War" (December 1936), Selected Works, Vol. I. p. 188.

24. CORRECTING MISTAKEN IDEAS

Even if we achieve gigantic successes in our work, there is no reason whatsoever to feel conceited and arrogant. Modesty helps one to go forward, whereas conceit makes one lag behind. This is a truth we must always bear in mind.

"Opening Address at the Eighth National Congress of the Communist Party of China" (September 15, 1956).

With victory, certain moods may grow within the Party--arrogance, the airs of a self-styled hero, inertia and unwillingness to make progress, love of pleasure and distaste for continued hard living. With victory, the people will be grateful to us and the bourgeoisie will come forward to flatter us. It has been proved that the enemy cannot conquer us by force of arms. However, the flattery of the bourgeoisie may conquer the weak-willed in our ranks. There may be some Communists, who were not conquered by enemies with guns and were worthy of the name of heroes for standing up to these enemies, but who cannot withstand sugar-coated bullets; they will be defeated by sugar-coated bullets. We must guard against such a situation.

"Report to the Second Plenary Session of the Seventh Central Committee of the Communist Party of China" (March 5, 1949), Selected Works, Vol. IV, p. 374.

Many things may become baggage, may become encumbrances if we cling to them blindly and uncritically. Let us take some illustrations. Having made mistakes, you may feel that, come what may, you are saddled with them and so become dispirited; if you have not made mistakes, you may feel that you are free from error and so become conceited. Lack of achievement in work may breed pessimism and depression, while achievement may breed pride and arrogance. A comrade with a short record of struggle may shirk responsibility on this account, while a veteran may become opinionated because of his long record of struggle. Worker and peasant comrades, because of pride in their class origin, may look down upon intellectuals, while intellectuals, because they have a certain amount of knowledge, may look down upon worker and peasant comrades. Any specialized skill may be capitalized on and so may lead to arrogance and contempt of others. Even one's age may become ground for conceit. The young, because they are bright and capable, may look down upon the old; and the old, because they are rich in experience, may look down upon the young. All such things become encumbrances or baggage if there is no critical awareness.

"Our Study and the Current Situation" (April 12, 1944), Selected Works, Vol. III, p. 173.

Some comrades in the army have become arrogant and high-handed in their behaviour towards the soldiers, the people, the government and the Party, always blaming the comrades doing local work but never themselves, always seeing their own achievements but never their own shortcomings, and always welcoming flattery but never criticism.... the army must endeavour to eradicate these faults.

"Get Organized!" (November 29, 1943), Selected Works, Vol. III, p. 159.

Hard work is like a load placed before us, challenging us to shoulder it. Some loads are light, some heavy. Some people prefer the light to the heavy; they pick the light and shove the heavy on to others. That is not a good attitude. Some comrades are different; they leave ease and comfort to others and take the heavy loads themselves; they are the first to bear hardships the last to enjoy comforts. They are good comrades. We should all learn from their communist spirit.

"On the Chungking Negotiations" (October 17, 1945), Selected Works, Vol. IV, p. 58.

There are not a few people who are irresponsible in their work, preferring the light to the heavy, shoving the heavy loads on to others and choosing the easy ones for themselves. At every turn they think of themselves before others. When they make some small contribution, they swell with pride and brag about it for fear that others will not know. They feel no warmth towards comrades and the people but are cold, indifferent and apathetic. In fact such people are not Communists, or at least cannot be counted as true Communists.

"In Memory of Norman Bethune" (December 21, 1939), Selected Works, Vol. II, pp. 337-38.

Those who assert this kind of "independence" are usually wedded to the doctrine of "me first" and are generally wrong on the question of the relationship between the individual and the Party. Although in words they profess respect for the Party, in practice they put themselves first and the Party second. What are these people after? They are after fame and position and want to be in the limelight. Whenever they are put in charge of a branch of work, they assert their "independence". With this aim, they draw some people in, push others out and resort to boasting, flattery and touting among the comrades, thus importing the vulgar style of the bourgeois political parties into the Communist Party. It is their dishonesty that causes them to come to grief. I believe we should do things honestly, for without an honest attitude it is absolutely impossible to accomplish anything in this world.

"Rectify the Party's Style of Work" (February 1, 1942), Selected Works, Vol. III, p. 44.

They [Communists] must grasp the principle of subordinating the needs of the part to the needs of the whole. If a proposal appears feasible for a partial situation but not for the situation as a whole, then the part must give way to the whole. Conversely, if the proposal is not feasible for the part but is feasible in the light of the situation as a whole, again the part must give way to the whole. This is what is meant by considering the situation as a whole.

"The Role of the Chinese Communist Party in the National War" (October 1938), Selected Works, Vol. II, p. 201.

Pleasure-seeking. In the Red Army there are also quite a few people whose individualism finds expression in pleasure-seeking. They always hope that their unit will march into big cities. They want to go there not to work but to enjoy themselves. The last thing they want is to work in the Red areas where life is hard.

"On Correcting Mistaken Ideas in the Party" (December 1929), Selected Works, Vol. I, p. 113.

We must oppose the tendency towards selfish departmentalism by which the interests of one's own unit are looked after to the exclusion of those of others. Whoever is indifferent to the difficulties of others, refuses to transfer cadres to other units on request, or releases only the inferior ones, "using the neighbour's field as an outlet for his overflow", and does not give the slightest consideration to other departments, localities or people--such a person is a selfish departmentalist who has entirely lost the spirit of communism. Lack of consideration for the whole and complete indifference to other departments, localities and people are characteristics of a selfish departmentalist. We must intensify our efforts to educate such persons and to make them understand that selfish departmentalism is a sectarian tendency which will become very dangerous, if allowed to develop.

"Rectify the Party's Style of Work" (February 1, 1942), Selected Works, Vol. III, p. 46.

Liberalism manifests itself in various ways.

To let things slide for the sake of peace and friendship when a person has clearly gone wrong, and refrain from principled argument because he is an old acquaintance, a fellow townsman, a schoolmate, a close friend, a loved one, an old colleague or old subordinate; or to touch on the matter lightly instead of going into it thoroughly, so as to keep on good terms--the result is that both the organization and the individual are harmed. This is one type of liberalism.

To indulge in irresponsible criticism in private, instead of actively putting forward one's suggestions to the organization; to say nothing to people to their faces but to gossip behind their backs, or to say nothing at a meeting but to gossip afterwards; to show no regard at all for the principles of collective life but to follow one's own inclination--this is a second type.

To let things drift if they do not affect one personally; to say as little as possible while knowing perfectly well what is wrong; to be worldly wise and play safe and seek only to avoid blame--this is a third type.

Not to obey orders but to give pride of place to one's own opinions; to demand special consideration from the organization but to reject its discipline--this is a fourth type.

To indulge in personal attacks, pick quarrels, vent personal spite or seek revenge instead of entering into an argument and struggling against incorrect views for the sake of unity or progress or getting the work done properly--this is a fifth type.

To hear incorrect views without rebutting them and even to hear counter-revolutionary remarks without reporting them, but instead to take them calmly as if nothing had happened--this is a sixth type.

To be among the masses and fail to conduct propaganda and agitation, or speak at meetings or conduct investigations and inquiries among them, and instead to be indifferent to them and show no concern for their well-being, forgetting that one is a Communist and behaving as if one were an ordinary non-Communist--this is a seventh type.

To see someone harming the interests of the masses and yet not feel indignant, or dissuade or stop him or reason with him, but to allow him to continue--this is an eighth type.

To work half-heartedly without a definite plan or direction; to work perfunctorily and muddle along--"So long as one remains a monk, one goes on tolling the bell"--this is a ninth type.

To regard oneself as having rendered great service to the revolution, to pride oneself on being a veteran, to disdain minor assignments while being quite unequal to major tasks, to be slipshod in work and slack in study--this is a tenth type.

To be aware of one's own mistakes and yet make no attempt to correct them, taking a liberal attitude towards oneself--this is an eleventh type.

"Combat Liberalism" (September 7, 1937), Selected Works, Vol. II, pp. 31-32.

Liberalism is extremely harmful in a revolutionary collective. It is a corrosive which eats away unity, undermines cohesion, causes apathy and creates dissension. It robs the revolutionary ranks of compact organization and strict discipline, prevents policies from being carried through and alienates the Party organizations from the masses which the Party leads. It is an extremely bad tendency.

Ibid. p. 32.

People who are liberals look upon the principles of Marxism as abstract dogma. They approve of Marxism, but are not prepared to practise it or to practise it in full; they are not prepared to replace their liberalism by Marxism. These people have their Marxism, but they have their liberalism as well--they talk Marxism but practise liberalism; they apply Marxism to others but liberalism to themselves. They keep both kinds of goods in stock and find a use for each. This is how the minds of certain people work.

Ibid. pp. 32-33

The people's state protects the people. Only when the people have such a state can they educate and remold themselves by democratic methods on a country-wide scale, with everyone taking part, and shake off the influence of domestic and foreign reactionaries (which is still very strong, will survive for a long time and cannot be quickly destroyed), rid themselves of the bad habits and ideas acquired in the old society, not allow themselves to be led astray by the reactionaries, and continue to advance--to advance towards a socialist and communist society.

"On the People's Democratic Dictatorship" (June 30, 1949). Selected Works, Vol. IV, p. 418.

It is not hard for one to do a bit of good. What is hard is to do good all one's life and never do anything bad, to act consistently in the interests of the broad masses, the young people and the revolution, and to engage in arduous struggle for decades on end. That is the hardest thing of all!

"Message of Greetings on the 60th Birthday of Comrade Wu Yu-chang" (January 15, 1940).

25. UNITY

The unification of our country, the unity of our people and the unity of our various nationalities--these are the basic guarantees of the sure triumph of our cause.

On the Correct Handling of Contradictions Among the People (February 27, 1957). 1st pocket ed., pp. 1-2.

It is only through the unity of the Communist Party that the unity of the whole class and the whole nation can be achieved, and it is only through the unity of the whole class and the whole nation that the enemy can be defeated and the national and democratic revolution accomplished.

"Win the Masses in Their Millions for the Anti-Japanese National United Front" (May 7, 1937), Selected Works, Vol. I, p. 292.

We shall solidly unite all the forces of our Party on democratic centralist principles of organization and discipline. We shall unite with any comrade if he abides by the Party's Programme, Constitution and decisions.

"On Coalition Government" (April 24, 1945), Selected Works, Vol. III, p. 317.

This democratic method of resolving contradictions among the people was epitomized in 1942 in the formula "unity, criticism, unity". To elaborate, it means starting from the desire for unity, resolving contradictions through criticism or struggle and arriving at a new unity on a new basis. In our experience this is the correct method of resolving contradictions among the people.

On the Correct Handling of Contradictions Among the People (February 27, 1957), 1st pocket ed., p. 12.

This [our] army has achieved remarkable unity in its own ranks and with those outside its ranks. Internally, there is unity between officers and men, between the higher and lower ranks, and between military work, political work and rear service work; and externally, there is unity between the army and the people, between the army and government organizations, and between our army and the friendly armies. It is imperative to overcome anything that impairs this unity.

"On Coalition Government" (April 24, 1945), Selected Works, Vol. III, p. 264.

26. DISCIPLINE

Within the ranks of the people, democracy is correlative with centralism and freedom with discipline. They are the two opposites of a single entity, contradictory as well as united, and we should not one-sidedly emphasize one to the denial of the other. Within the ranks of the people, we cannot do without freedom, nor can we do without discipline; we cannot do without democracy, nor can we do without centralism. This unity of democracy and centralism, of freedom and discipline, constitutes our democratic centralism. Under this system, the people enjoy extensive democracy and freedom, but at the same time they have to keep within the bounds of socialist discipline.

On the Correct Handling of Contradictions Among the People (February 27, 1957), 1st pocket ed., pp. 10-11.

We must affirm anew the discipline of the Party, namely:
(1) the individual is subordinate to the organization;
(2) the minority is subordinate to the majority;
(3) the lower level is subordinate to the higher level; and
(4) the entire membership is subordinate to the Central Committee.

Whoever violates these articles of discipline disrupts Party unity.

"The Role of the Chinese Communist Party in the National War" (October 1938), Selected Works, Vol. II, pp. 203-04.

One requirement of Party discipline is that the minority should submit to the majority. If the view of the minority has been rejected, it must support the decision passed by the majority. If necessary, it can bring up the matter for reconsideration at the next meeting, but apart from that it must not act against the decision in any way.

"On Correcting Mistaken Ideas in the Party" (December 1929), Selected Works, Vol. I, p. 110.

The Three Main Rules of Discipline are as follows:

(1) Obey orders in all your actions.
(2) Do not take a single needle piece of thread from the masses.
(3) Turn in everything captured.

The Eight Points for Attention are as follows:

(1) Speak politely.
(2) Pay fairly for what you buy.
(3) Return everything you borrow.
(4) Pay for anything you damage.
(5) Do not hit or swear at people.
(6) Do not damage crops.
(7) Do not take liberties with women.

(8) Do not ill-treat captives.

"On the Reissue of the Three Main Rules of Discipline and the Eight Points for Attention--Instruction of the General Headquarters of the Chinese People's Liberation Army" (October 10, 1947), Selected Military Writings, 2nd ed., p. 343.

They [all officers and soldiers of our army] must heighten their sense of discipline and resolutely carry out orders, carry out our policy, carry out the Three Main Rules of Discipline and the Eight Points for Attention--with army and people united, army and government united, officers and soldiers united, and the whole army united--and permit no breach of discipline.

"Manifesto of the Chinese People's Liberation Army" (October 1947), Selected Military Writings, 2nd ed., p. 340.

27. CRITICISM AND SELF-CRITICISM

The Communist Party does not fear criticism because we are Marxists, the truth is on our side, and the basic masses, the workers and peasants are on our side.

Speech at the Chinese Communist Party's National Conference on Propaganda Work (March 12, 1957), 1st pocket ed., p. 14.

Thoroughgoing materialists are fearless; we hope that all our fellow fighters will courageously shoulder their responsibilities and overcome all difficulties, fearing no setbacks or gibes, nor hesitating to criticize us Communists and give us their suggestions. "He who is not afraid of death by a thousand cuts dares to unhorse the emperor"--this is the indomitable spirit needed in our struggle to build socialism and communism.

Ibid. p. 16.

We have the Marxist-Leninist weapon of criticism and self-criticism. We can get tide of a bad style and keep the good.

"Report to the Second Plenary Session of the Seventh Central Committee of the Communist Party of China" (March 5, 1949), Selected Works, Vol. IV, p. 374.

Conscientious practice of self-criticism is still another hallmark distinguishing our Party from all other political parties. As we say, dust will accumulate if a room is not cleaned regularly, our faces will get dirty if they are not washed regularly. Our comrades' minds and our Party's work may also collect dust, and also need sweeping and washing. The proverb, "Running water is never stale and a door-hinge is never worm-eaten", means that constant motion prevents the inroads of germs and other organisms. To check up regularly on our work and in the process develop a democratic style of work, to fear neither criticism nor self-criticism, and to apply such good popular Chinese maxims as "Say all you know and say it without reserve", "Blame not the speaker but be warned by his words" and "Correct mistakes if you have committed them and guard against them if you have not"--this is the only effective way to prevent all kinds of political dust and germs from contaminating the minds of our comrades and the body of our Party.

"On Coalition Government" (April 24, 1945), Selected Works, Vol. III, pp. 316-17.

Opposition and struggle between ideas of different kinds constantly occur within the Party; this is a reflection within the Party of contradictions between classes and between the new and the old in society. If there were no contradictions in the Party and no ideological struggles to resolve them, the Party's life would come to an end.

"On Contradiction" (August 1937), Selected Works, Vol. I, p. 317.

We stand for active ideological struggle because it is the weapon for ensuring unity within the Party and the revolutionary organizations in the interest of our fight. Every Communist and revolutionary should take up this weapon.

But liberalism rejects ideological struggle and stands for unprincipled peace, thus giving rise to a decadent, philistine attitude and bringing about political degeneration in certain units and individuals in the Party and the revolutionary organizations.

"Combat Liberalism" (September 7, 1937), Selected Works, Vol. II, p. 31.

In opposing subjectivism, sectarianism and stereotyped Party writing we must have in mind two purposes: first, "learn from past mistakes to avoid future ones", and second, "cure the sickness to save the patient". The mistakes of the past must be exposed without sparing anyone's sensibilities; it is necessary to analyse and criticize what was bad in the past with a scientific attitude so that work in the future will be done more carefully and done better. This is what is meant by "learn from past mistakes to avoid future ones". But our aim in exposing errors and criticizing shortcomings, like that of a doctor curing a sickness, is solely to save the patient and not to doctor him to death. A person with appendicitis is saved when the surgeon removes his appendix. So long as a person who has made mistakes does not hide his sickness for fear of treatment or persist in his mistakes until he is beyond cure, so long as he honestly and sincerely wishes to be cured and to mend his ways, we should welcome him and cure his sickness so that he can become a good comrade. We can never succeed if we just let ourselves go and lash out at him. In treating an ideological or a political malady, one must never be rough and rash but must adopt the approach of "curing the sickness to save the patient", which is the only correct and effective method.

"Rectify the Party's Style of Work" (February 1, 1942), Selected Works, Vol. III, p. 50.

Another point that should be mentioned in connection with inner-Party criticism is that some comrades ignore the major issues and confine their attention to minor points when they make their criticism. They do not understand that the main task of criticism is to point out political and organizational mistakes. As to personal shortcomings, unless they are related to political and organizational mistakes, there is no need to be overcritical or the comrades concerned will be at a loss as to what to do. Moreover, once such criticism develops, there is the great danger that within the Party attention will be concentrated exclusively on minor faults, and everyone will become timid and overcautious and forget the Party's political tasks.

"On Correcting Mistaken Ideas in the Party" (December 1929), Selected Works, Vol. I, pp. 111-12.

In inner-Party criticism, guard against subjectivism, arbitrariness and the vulgarization of criticism; statements should be based on facts and criticism should stress the political side.

Ibid. p. 112.

Inner-Party criticism is a weapon for strengthening the Party organization and increasing its fighting capacity. In the Party organization of the Red Army, however, criticism is not always of this character, and sometimes turns into personal attack. As a result, it damages the Party organization as well as individuals. This is a manifestation of petty-bourgeois individualism. The method of correction is to help Party members understand that the purpose of criticism is to increase the Party's fighting capacity in order to achieve victory in the class struggle and that it should not be used as a means of personal attack.

Ibid. p. 110.

If we have shortcomings, we are not afraid to have them pointed out and criticized, because we serve the people. Anyone, no matter who, may point out our shortcomings. If he is right, we will correct them. If what he proposes will benefit the people, we will act upon it.

"Serve the People" (September 8, 1941), Selected Works, Vol. III, P. 227.

As we Chinese Communists, who base all our actions on the highest interests of the broadest masses of the Chinese people and who are fully convinced of the justice of our cause, never balk at any personal sacrifice and are ready at all times to give our lives for the cause, can we be reluctant to discard any idea, viewpoint, opinion or method which is not suited to the needs of the people? Can we be willing to allow political dust and germs to dirty our clean faces or eat into our healthy organisms? Countless revolutionary martyrs have laid down their lives in the interests of the people, and our hearts are filled with pain as we the living think of them--can there be any personal interest, then, that we would not sacrifice or any error that we would not discard?

"On Coalition Government" (April 24, 1945), Selected Works, Vol. III, p. 317.

We must not become complacent over any success. We should check our complacency and constantly criticize our shortcomings, just as we should wash our faces or sweep the floor every day to remove the dirt and keep them clean.

"Get Organized!" (November 29, 1943), Selected Works, Vol. III. p. 160.

As for criticism, do it in good time; don't get into the habit of criticizing only after the event.
On the Question of Agricultural Co-operation (July 31, 1955), 3rd ed., p. 25.

Taught by mistakes and setbacks, we have become wiser and handle our affairs better. It is hard for any political party or person to avoid mistakes, but we should make as few as possible. Once a mistake is made, we should correct it, and the more quickly and thoroughly the better.

"On the People's Democratic Dictatorship" (June 30, 1949), Selected Works, Vol. IV, p. 422.

28. COMMUNISTS

A Communist should have largeness of mind and he should be staunch and active, looking upon the interests of the revolution as his very life and subordinating his personal interests to those of the revolution; always and everywhere he should adhere to principle and wage a tireless struggle against all incorrect ideas and actions, so as to consolidate the collective life of the Party and strengthen the ties between the Party and the masses; he should be more concerned about the Party and the masses than about any individual, and more concerned about others than about himself. Only thus can he be considered a Communist.

"Combat Liberalism" (September 7, 1937), Selected Works, Vol. II, p. 33.

Every comrade must be brought to understand that the supreme test of the words and deeds of a Communist is whether they conform with the highest interests and enjoy the support of the overwhelming majority of the people.

"On Coalition Government" (April 24, 1945), Selected Works, Vol. III, p. 316.

At no time and in no circumstances should a Communist place his personal interests first; he should subordinate them to the interests of the nation and of the masses. Hence, selfishness, slacking, corruption, seeking the limelight, and so on, are most contemptible, while selflessness, working with all one's energy, whole-hearted devotion to public duty, and quiet hard work will command respect.

"The Role of the Chinese Communist Party in the National War" (October 1938), Selected Works, Vol. II, p. 198.

Communists must be ready at all times to stand up for the truth, because truth is in the interests of the people; Communists must be ready at all times to correct their mistakes, because mistakes are against the interests of the people.

"On Coalition Government" (April 24, 1945), Selected Works, Vol. III, p. 315.

Communists must always go into the whys and wherefores of anything, use their own heads and carefully think over whether or not it corresponds to reality and is really well founded; on no account should they follow blindly and encourage slavishness.

"Rectify the Party's Style of Work" (February 1, 1942), Selected Works, Vol. III, pp. 49-50.

We should encourage comrades to take the interests of the whole into account. Every Party member, every branch of work, every statement and every action must proceed from the interests of the whole Party; it is absolutely impermissible to violate this principle.

Ibid. p. 44.

Communists should set an example in being practical as well as far-sighted. For only by being practical can they fulfill the appointed tasks, and only far-sightedness can prevent them from losing their bearings in the march forward.

"The Role of the Chinese Communist Party in the National War" (October 1938), Selected Works, Vol. II, p. 198.

Communists should be the most farsighted, the most self-sacrificing, the most resolute, and the least prejudiced in sizing up situations, and should rely on the majority of the masses and win their support.

"The Tasks of the Chinese Communist Party in the Period of Resistance to Japan" (May 3, 1937), Selected Works, Vol. I, p. 274.

Communists should set an example in study; at all times they should be pupils of the masses as well as their teachers.

"The Role of the Chinese Communist Party in the National War" (October 1938), Selected Works, Vol. II, p. 198.
Every Communist working in the mass movements should be a friend of the masses and not a boss over them, an indefatigable teacher and not a bureaucratic politician.

Ibid.

Communists must never separate themselves from the majority of the people or neglect them by leading only a few progressive contingents in an isolated and rash advance, but must take care to forge close links between the progressive elements and the broad masses. This is what is meant by thinking in terms of the majority.

Ibid. p. 201.

We Communists are like seeds and the people are like the soil. Wherever we go, we must unite with the people, take root and blossom among them.

"On the Chungking Negotiations" (October 17, 1945), Selected Works, Vol. IV, p. 58.

We Communists must be able to integrate ourselves with the masses in all things. If our Party members spend their whole lives sitting indoors and never go out to face the world and brave the storm, what good will they be to the Chinese people? None at all, and we do not need such people as Party members. We Communists ought to face the world and brave the storm the great world of mass struggle and the mighty storm of mass struggle.

"Get Organized!" (November 29, 1943), Selected Works, Vol. III, p. 158.

The exemplary vanguard role of the Communists is of vital importance. Communists in the Eighth Route and New Fourth Armies should set an example in fighting bravely, carrying out orders, observing discipline, doing political work and fostering internal unity and solidarity.

"The Role of the Chinese Communist Party in the National War" (October 1938), *Selected Works, Vol. II, p. 197.*

A Communist must never be opinionated or domineering, thinking that he is good in everything while others are good in nothing; he must never shut himself up in his little room, or brag and boast and lord it over others.

"Speech at the Assembly of Representatives of the Shensi-Kansu-Ningsia Border Region" *(November 21, 1941), Selected Works, Vol. III, p. 33.*

Communists must listen attentively to the views of people outside the Party and let them have their say. If what they say is right, we ought to welcome it, and we should learn from their strong points; if it is wrong, we should let them finish what they are saying and then patiently explain things to them.

Ibid.

The attitude of Communists towards any person who has made mistakes in his work should be one of persuasion in order to help him change and start afresh and not one of exclusion, unless he is incorrigible.

"The Role of the Chinese Communist Party in the National War" (October 1938), *Selected Works, Vol. II, p. 198.*

As for people who are politically backward, Communists should not slight or despise them, but should befriend them, unite with them, convince them and encourage them to go forward.

Ibid.

29. CADRES

In order to guarantee that our Party and country do not change their colour, we must not only have a correct line and correct policies, but must train and bring up millions of successors who will carry on the cause of proletarian revolution.

In the final analysis, the question of training successors for the revolutionary cause of the proletariat is one of whether or not there will be people who can carry on the Marxist-Leninist revolutionary cause started by the older generation of proletarian revolutionaries, whether or not the leadership of our Party and state will remain in the hands of proletarian revolutionaries, whether or not our descendants will continue to march along the correct road laid down by Marxism-Leninism, or, in other words, whether or not we can successfully prevent the emergence of Khrushchov's revisionism in China. In short, it is an extremely important question, a matter of life and death for our Party and our country. It is a question of fundamental importance to the proletarian revolutionary cause for a hundred, a thousand, nay ten thousand years. Basing themselves on the changes in the Soviet Union, the imperialist prophets are pinning their hopes of "peaceful evolution" on the third or fourth generation of the Chinese Party. We must shatter these imperialist prophecies. From our highest organizations down to the grassroots, we must everywhere give constant attention to the training and upbringing of successors to the revolutionary cause.

What are the requirements for worthy successors to the revolutionary cause of the proletariat?

They must be genuine Marxist-Leninists and not revisionists like Khrushchov wearing the cloak of Marxism-Leninism.

They must be revolutionaries who wholeheartedly serve the overwhelming majority of the people of China and the whole world, and must not be like Khrushchov who serves both the interests of the handful of members of the privileged bourgeois stratum in his own country and those of foreign imperialism and reaction.

They must be proletarian statesmen capable of uniting and working together with the overwhelming majority. Not only must they unite with those who agree with them, they must also be good at uniting with those who disagree and even with those who formerly opposed them and have since been proved wrong in practice. But they must especially watch out for careerists and conspirators like Khrushchov and prevent such bad elements from usurping the leadership of the Party and the state at any level.

They must be models in applying the Party's democratic centralism, must master the method of leadership based on the principle of "from the masses, to the masses", and must cultivate a democratic style and be good at listening to the masses. They must not be despotic like Khrushchov and violate the Party's democratic centralism, make surprise attacks on comrades or act arbitrarily and dictatorially.

They must be modest and prudent and guard against arrogance and impetuosity; they must be imbued with the spirit of self-criticism and have the courage to correct mistakes and shortcomings in their work. They must never cover up their errors like Khrushchov, and claim all the credit for themselves and shift all the blame on others.

Successors to the revolutionary cause of the proletariat come forward in mass struggles and are tempered in the great storms of revolution. It is essential to test and judge cadres and choose and train successors in the long course of mass struggle.

Quoted in On Khrushchov's Phoney Communism and Its Historical Lessons for the World (July 14,1964), pp. 72-74.

Our Party organizations must be extended all over the country and we must purposefully train tens of thousands of cadres and hundreds of first-rate mass leaders. They must be cadres and leaders versed in Marxism-Leninism, politically far-sighted, competent in work, full of the spirit of self-sacrifice, capable of tackling problems on their own, steadfast in the midst of difficulties and loyal and devoted in serving the nation, the class and the Party. It is on these cadres and leaders that the Party relies for its links with the membership and the masses, and it is by relying on their firm leadership of the masses that the Party can succeed in defeating the enemy. Such cadres and leaders must be free from selfishness, from individualistic heroism, ostentation, sloth, passivity, and arrogant sectarianism, and they must be selfless national and class heroes; such are the qualities and the style of work demanded of the members, cadres and leaders of our Party.

"Win the Masses in Their Millions for the Anti-Japanese National United Front" (May 7, 1937), Selected Works, Vol. I, p. 291.

Cadres are a decisive factor, once the political line is determined. Therefore, it is our fighting task to train large numbers of new cadres in a planned way.

"The Role of the Chinese Communist Party in the National War" (October 1938), Selected Works, Vol. II, p. 202.

The criterion the Communist Party should apply in its cadres policy is whether or not a cadre is resolute in carrying out the Party line, keeps to Party discipline, has close ties with the masses, has the ability to find his bearings independently, and is active, hardworking and unselfish. This is what "appointing people on their merit" means.

Ibid.

It is necessary to maintain the system of cadre participation in collective productive labour. The cadres of our Party and state are ordinary workers and not overlords sitting on the backs of the people. By taking part in collective productive labour, the cadres maintain extensive, constant and close ties with the working people. This is a major measure of fundamental importance for a socialist system; it helps to overcome bureaucracy and to prevent revisionism and dogmatism.

Quoted in On Khrushchov's Phoney Communism and Its Historical Lessons for the World (July 14, 1964), pp. 68-69.

We must know how to judge cadres. We must not confine our judgment to a short period or a single incident in a cadre's life, but should consider his life and work as a whole. This is the principal method of judging cadres.

"The Role of the Chinese Communist Party in the National War" (October 1938), Selected Works, Vol. II, p. 202.

We must, know how to use cadres well. In the final analysis, leadership involves two main responsibilities: to work out ideas, and to use cadres well. Such things as drawing up plans, making decisions, and giving orders and directives, are all in the category of "working out ideas". To put the ideas into practice, we must weld the cadres together and encourage them to go into action; this comes into the category of "using the cadres well".

Ibid.

We must know how to take good care of cadres. There are several ways of doing so.

First, give them guidance. This means allowing them a free hand in their work so that they have the courage to assume responsibility and, at the same time, giving them timely instructions so that, guided by the Party's political line, they are able to make full use of their initiative.
Second, raise their level. This means educating them by giving them the opportunity to study so that they can enhance their theoretical understanding and their working ability.

Third, check up on their work, and help them sum up their experience, carry forward their achievements and correct their mistakes. To assign work without checking up and to take notice only when serious mistakes are made--that is not the way to take care of cadres.

Fourth, in general, use the method of persuasion with cadres who have made mistakes, and help them correct their mistakes. The method of struggle should be confined to those who make serious mistakes and nevertheless refuse to accept guidance. Here patience is essential. It is wrong lightly to label people "opportunists" or lightly to begin "waging struggles" against them.

Fifth, help them with their difficulties. When cadres are in difficulty as a result of illness, straitened means or domestic or other troubles, we must be sure to give them as much care as possible.

This is how to take good care of cadres.

Ibid. p. 203.

A leading group that is genuinely united and is linked with the masses can gradually be formed only in the process of mass struggle, and not in isolation from it. In the process of a great struggle, the composition of the leading group in most cases should not and cannot remain entirely unchanged throughout the initial, middle and final stages; the activists who come forward in the course of the struggle must constantly be promoted to replace those original members of the leading group who are inferior by comparison or who have degenerated.

"Some Questions Concerning Methods of Leadership" (June 1, 1943), Selected Works, Vol. III, p. 118.

If our Party does not have a great many new cadres working in unity and cooperation with the old cadres, our cause will come to a stop. All old cadres, therefore, should welcome the new ones with the utmost enthusiasm and show them the warmest solicitude. True, new cadres have their shortcomings. They have not been long in the revolution and lack experience, and unavoidably some have brought with them vestiges of the unwholesome ideology of the old society, remnants of the ideology of petty-bourgeois individualism. But such shortcomings can be gradually eliminated through education and tempering in the revolution. The strong point of the new cadres, as Stalin has said, is that they are acutely sensitive to what is new and are therefore enthusiastic and active to a high degree--the very qualities which some of the old cadres lack. Cadres, new and old, should respect each other, learn from each other and overcome their own shortcomings by learning from each other's strong points, so as to unite as one in the common cause and guard against sectarian tendencies.

"Rectify the Party's Style of Work" (February 1, 1942), Selected Works, Vol. III, p. 47.

Our concern should extend to non-Party cadres as well as to Party cadres. There are many capable people outside the Party whom we must not ignore. The duty of every Communist is to rid himself of aloofness and arrogance and to work well with non-Party cadres, give them sincere help, have a warm, comradely attitude towards them and enlist their initiative in the great cause of resisting Japan and reconstructing the nation.

"The Role of the Chinese Communist Party in the National War" (October 1938), Selected Works, Vol. II, p. 202.

30. YOUTH

The world is yours, as well as ours, but in the last analysis, it is yours. You young people, full of vigour and vitality, are in the bloom of life, like the sun at eight or nine in the morning. Our hope is placed on you.

The world belongs to you. China's future belongs to you.

Talk at a meeting with Chinese students and trainees in Moscow (November 17, 1957).

We must help all our young people to understand that ours is still a very poor country, that we cannot change this situation radically in a short time, and that only through the united efforts of our younger generation and all our people, working with their own hands, can China be made strong and prosperous within a period of several decades. The establishment of our socialist system has opened the road leading to the ideal society of the future, but to translate this ideal into reality needs hard work.

On the Correct Handling of Contradictions Among the People (February 27, 1957), 1st pocket ed., pp. 44-45.

Because of their lack of political and social experience, quite a number of young people are unable to see the contrast between the old China and the new, and it is not easy for them thoroughly to comprehend the hardships our people went through in the struggle to free themselves from the oppression of the imperialists and Kuomintang reactionaries, or the long period of arduous work needed before a happy socialist society can be established. That is why we must constantly carry on lively and effective political education among the masses and should always tell them the truth about the difficulties that crop up and discuss with them how to surmount these difficulties.

Ibid. p. 63.

The young people are the most active and vital force in society. They are the most eager to learn and the least conservative in their thinking. This is especially so in the era of socialism. We hope that the local Party organizations in various places will help and work with the Youth League organizations and go into the question of bringing into full play the energy of our youth in particular. The Party organizations should not treat them in the same way as everybody else and ignore their special characteristics. Of course, the young people should learn from the old and other adults, and should strive as much as possible to engage in all sorts of useful activities with their agreement.

Introductory note to "A Youth Shock Brigade of the No. 9 Agricultural Producers' Co-operative in Hsinping Township, Chungshan County" (1955), The Socialist Upsurge in China's Countryside, Chinese ed., Vol. III.

How should we judge whether a youth is a revolutionary? How can we tell? There can only be one criterion, namely, whether or not he is willing to integrate himself with the broad masses of workers and peasants and does so in practice. If he is willing to do so and actually does so, he is a revolutionary; otherwise he is a non-revolutionary or a counter-revolutionary. If today he integrates himself with the masses of workers and peasants, then today he is a revolutionary; if tomorrow he ceases to do so or turns round to oppress the common people, then he becomes a non-revolutionary or a counter-revolutionary.

"The Orientation of the Youth Movement" (May 4, 1939), Selected Works, Vol. II, p. 246.

The intellectuals often tend to be subjective and individualistic, impractical in their thinking and irresolute in action until they have thrown themselves heart and soul into mass revolutionary struggles, or made up their minds to serve the interests of the masses and become one with them. Hence although the mass of revolutionary intellectuals in China can play a vanguard role or serve as a link with the masses, not all of them will remain revolutionaries to the end. Some will drop out of the revolutionary ranks at critical moments and become passive, while a few may even become enemies of the revolution. The intellectuals can overcome their shortcomings only in mass struggles over a long period.

"The Chinese Revolution and the Chinese Communist Party" (December 1939), Selected Works, Vol. II, p. 322.

Apart from continuing to act in co-ordination with the Party in its central task, the Youth League should do its own work to suit the special characteristics of youth. New China must care for her youth and show concern for the growth of the younger generation. Young people have to study and work, but they are at the age of physical growth. Therefore, full attention must be paid both to their work and study and to their recreation, sport and rest.

Talk at the reception for the Presidium of the Second National Congress of the Youth League (June 30, 1953).

31. WOMEN

A man in China is usually subjected to the domination of three systems of authority [political authority, clan authority and religious authority]. As for women, in addition to being dominated by these three systems of authority they are also dominated by the men (the authority of the husband). These four authorities--political, clan, religious and masculine--are the embodiment of the whole feudal-patriarchal ideology and system, and are the four thick ropes binding the Chinese people, particularly the peasants. How the peasants have overthrown the political authority of the landlords in the countryside has been described above. The political authority of the landlords is the backbone of all the other systems of authority. With that overturned, the clan authority, the religious authority and the authority of the husband all begin to totter. As to the authority of the husband, this has always been weaker among the poor peasants because, out of economic necessity, their womenfolk have to do more manual labour than the women of the richer classes and therefore have more say and greater power of decision in family matters. With the increasing bankruptcy of the rural economy in recent years, the basis for men's domination over women has already been undermined. With the rise of the peasant movement, the women in many places have now begun to organize rural women's associations; the opportunity has come for them to lift up their heads, and the authority of the husband is getting shakier every day. In a word, the whole feudal-patriarchal ideology and system is tottering with the growth of the peasants' power.

"Report on an Investigation of the Peasant Movement in Hunan" (March 1927), Selected Works, Vol. I, pp. 44-46.

Unite and take part in production and political activity to improve the economic and political status of women.

Inscription for the magazine, Women of New China, printed in its first issue, July 20, 1949.

Protect the interests of the youth, women and children--provide assistance to young students who cannot afford to continue their studies, help the youth and women to organize in order to participate on an equal footing in all work useful to the war effort and to social progress, ensure freedom of marriage and equality as between men and women, and give young people and children a useful education.

"On Coalition Government" (April 24, 1945), Selected Works, Vol. III, p. 288.

[In agricultural production] our fundamental task is to adjust the use of labour power in an organized way and to encourage women to do farm work.

"Our Economic Policy" (January 23, 1934), Selected Works, Vol. I, p. 142.

In order to build a great socialist society it is of the utmost importance to arouse the broad masses of women to join in productive activity. Men and women must receive equal pay for equal work in production. Genuine equality between the sexes can only be realized in the process of the socialist transformation of society as a whole.

Introductory note to "Women Have Gone to the Labour Front" (1955), The Socialist Upsurge in China's Countryside, Chinese ed., Vol. I.

With the completion of agricultural cooperation, many co-operatives are finding themselves short of labour. It has become necessary to arouse the great mass of women who did not work in the fields before to take their place on the labour front. China's women are a vast reserve of labour power. This reserve should be tapped in the struggle to build a great socialist country.

Introductory note to "Solving the Labour Shortage by Arousing the Women to Join in Production" (1955), The Socialist Upsurge in China's Countryside, Chinese ed., Vol. II.

Enable every woman who can work to take her place on the labour front, under the principle of equal pay for equal work. This should be done as quickly as possible.

Introductory note to "On Widening the Scope of Women's Work in the Agricultural Co-operative Movement" (1955), The Socialist Upsurge in China's Countryside, Chinese ed., Vol. I.

32. CULTURE AND ART

In the world today all culture, all literature and art belong to definite classes and are geared to definite political lines. There is in fact no such thing as art for art's sake, art that stands above classes, art that is detached from or independent of politics. Proletarian literature and art are part of the whole proletarian revolutionary cause; they are, as Lenin said, cogs and wheels in the whole revolutionary machine.

"Talks at the Yenan Forum on Literature and Art" (May 1942), Selected Works, Vol. III, p. 86.

Revolutionary culture is a powerful revolutionary weapon for the broad masses of the people. It prepares the ground ideologically before the revolution comes and is an important, indeed essential, fighting front in the general revolutionary front during the revolution.

"On New Democracy" (January 1940), Selected Works, Vol. II, p. 382.

All our literature and art are for the masses of the people, and in the first place for the workers, peasants and soldiers; they are created for the workers, peasants and soldiers and are for their use.

"Talks at the Yenan Forum on Literature and Art" (May 1942), Selected Works, Vol. III, p. 84.

Our literary and art workers must accomplish this task and shift their stand; they must gradually move their feet over to the side of the workers, peasants and soldiers, to the side of the proletariat, through the process of going into their very midst and into the thick of practical struggles and through the process of studying Marxism and society. Only in this way can we have a literature and art that are truly for the workers, peasants and soldiers, a truly proletarian literature and art.

Ibid. p. 78.

[Our purpose is] to ensure that literature and art fit well into the whole revolutionary machine as a component part, that they operate as powerful weapons for uniting and educating the people and for attacking and destroying the enemy, and that they help the people fight the enemy with one heart and one mind.

Ibid. p. 70.

In literary and art criticism there are two criteria, the political and the artistic.

There is the political criterion and there is the artistic criterion; what is the relationship between the two? Politics cannot be equated with art, nor can a general world outlook be equated with a method of artistic creation and criticism. We deny not only that there is an abstract and absolutely unchangeable political criterion, but also that there is an abstract and absolutely unchangeable artistic criterion; each class in every class society has its own political and artistic criteria. But all classes in all class societies invariably put the political criterion first and the artistic criterion second. What we demand is the unity of politics and art, the unity of content and form, the unity of revolutionary political content and the highest possible perfection of artistic form. Works of art which lack artistic quality have no force, however progressive they are politically. Therefore, we oppose both works of art with a wrong political viewpoint and the tendency towards the "poster and slogan style" which is correct in political viewpoint but lacking in artistic power. On questions of literature and art we must carry on a struggle on two fronts.

Ibid. pp. 88-90.

Letting a hundred flowers blossom and a hundred schools of thought contend is the policy for promoting the progress of the arts and the sciences and a flourishing socialist culture in our land. Different forms and styles in art should develop freely and different schools in science should contend freely. We think that it is harmful to the growth of art and science if administrative measures are used to impose one particular style of art or school of thought and to ban another. Questions of right and wrong in the arts and sciences should be settled through free discussion in artistic and scientific circles and through practical work in these fields. They should not be settled in summary fashion.

On the Correct Handling of Contradictions Among the People (February 27, 1957), 1st pocket ed., pp. 49-50.

An army without culture is a dull-witted army, and a dull-witted army cannot defeat the enemy.

"The United Front in Cultural Work" (October 30, 1944), Selected Works, Vol. III, p. 235.

33. STUDY

In transforming a backward agricultural China into an advanced industrialized country, we are confronted with arduous tasks and our experience is far from adequate. So we must be good at learning.

"Opening Address at the Eighth National Congress of the Communist Party of China" (September 15, 1956).

Conditions are changing all the time, and to adapt one's thinking to the new conditions, one must study. Even those who have a better grasp of Marxism and are comparatively firm in their proletarian stand have to go on studying, have to absorb what is new and study new problems.

Speech at the Chinese Communist Party's National Conference on Propaganda Work (March 12, 1957), 1st pocket ed., p. 8.

We can learn what we did not know. We are not only good at destroying the old world--we are also good at building the new.

"Report to the Second Plenary Session of the Seventh Central Committee of the Communist Party of China" (March 5, 1949), Selected Works, Vol. IV, p. 374.

Now, there are two different attitudes towards learning from others. One is the dogmatic attitude of transplanting everything, whether or not it is suited to our conditions. This is no good. The other attitude is to use our heads and learn those things which suit our conditions, that is, to absorb whatever experience is useful to us. That is the attitude we should adopt.

On the Correct Handling of Contradictions Among the People (February 27, 1957), 1st pocket ed., p. 75.

The theory of Marx, Engels, Lenin and Stalin is universally applicable. We should regard it not as a dogma, but as a guide to action. Studying it is not merely a matter of learning terms and phrases but of learning Marxism-Leninism as the science of revolution. It is not just a matter of understanding the general laws derived by Marx, Engels, Lenin and Stalin from their extensive study of real life and revolutionary experience, but of studying their standpoint and method in examining and solving problems.

"The Role of the Chinese Communist Party in the National War" (October 1938), Selected Works, Vol. II, pp. 208-09.

If we have a correct theory but merely prate about it, pigeonhole it and do not put it into practice, then that theory, however good, is of no significance.

"On Practice" (July 1937), Selected Works, Vol. I, p. 304.

It is necessary to master Marxist theory and apply it, master it for the sole purpose of applying it. If you can apply the Marxist-Leninist viewpoint in elucidating one or two practical problems, you should be commended and credited with some achievement. The more problems you elucidate and the more comprehensively and profoundly you do so, the greater will be your achievement.

"Rectify the Party's Style of Work" (February 1, 1942), Selected Works, Vol. III, p. 38.

How is Marxist-Leninist theory to be linked with the practice of the Chinese revolution? To use a common expression, it is by "shooting the arrow at the target". As the arrow is to the target, so is Marxism-Leninism to the Chinese revolution. Some comrades, however, are "shooting without a target", shooting at random, and such people are liable to harm the revolution.

Ibid. p. 42.

Those experienced in work must take up the study of theory and must read seriously; only then will they be able to systematize and synthesize their experience and raise it to the level of theory, only then will they not mistake their partial experience for universal truth and not commit empiricist errors.

Ibid.

Reading is learning, but applying is also learning and the more important kind of learning at that. Our chief method is to learn warfare through warfare. A person who has had no opportunity to go to school can also learn warfare--he can learn through fighting in war. A revolutionary war is a mass undertaking; it is often not a matter of first learning and then doing, but of doing and then learning, for doing is itself learning.

"Problems of Strategy in China's Revolutionary War" (December 1936), Selected Works, Vol. I, pp. 189-90.

There is a gap between the ordinary civilian and the soldier, but it is no Great Wall, and it can be quickly closed, and the way to close it is to take part in revolution, in war. By saying that it is not easy to learn and to apply, we mean that it is hard to learn thoroughly and to apply skillfully. By saying that civilians can very quickly become soldiers, we mean that it is not difficult to cross the threshold. To put the two statements together, we may cite the Chinese adage: "Nothing in the world is difficult for one who sets his mind to it." To cross the threshold is not difficult, and mastery, too, is possible provided one sets one's mind to the task and is good at learning.

Ibid. p. 190.

We must learn to do economic work from all who know how, no matter who they are. We must esteem them as teachers, learning from them respectfully and conscientiously. We must not pretend to know when we do not know.

"On the People's Democratic Dictatorship" (June 30, 1949), Selected Works, Vol. IV, p. 423.

Knowledge is a matter of science, and no dishonesty or conceit whatsoever is permissible. What is required is definitely the reverse-- honesty and modesty.

"On Practice" (July 1937), Selected Works, Vol. I, p. 300.

Complacency is the enemy of study. We cannot really learn anything until we rid ourselves of complacency. Our attitude towards ourselves should be "to be insatiable in learning" and towards others "to be tireless in teaching".

"The Role of the Chinese Communist Party in the National War" (October 1938), Selected Works, Vol. II, p. 210.

Some people have read a few Marxist books and think themselves quite learned but what they have read has not penetrated, has not struck root in their minds, so that they do not know how to use it and their class feelings remain as of old. Others are very conceited and having learned some book-phrases, think themselves terrific and are very cocky; but whenever a storm blows up, they take a stand very different from that of the workers and the majority of the peasants. They waver while the latter stand firm; they equivocate while the latter are forthright.

Speech at the Chinese Communist Party's National Conference on Propaganda Work (March 12, 1957), 1st pocket ed., pp. 7-8.

In order to have a real grasp of Marxism, one must learn it not only from books, but mainly through class struggle, through practical work and close contact with the masses of workers and peasants. When in addition to reading some Marxist books our intellectuals have gained some understanding through close contact with the masses of workers and peasants and through their own practical work, we will all be speaking the same language, not only the common language of patriotism and the common language of the socialist system, but probably even the common language of the communist world outlook. If that happens, all of us will certainly work much better.

Ibid. p. 12.

BN Publishing

Improving People's Life

www.bnpublishing.com

CPSIA information can be obtained at www.ICGtesting.com
Printed in the USA
LVOW03s2127210915

455165LV00006B/47/P